Karen Holding
—✗— —✗—

Karen Holding
—✗— —✗—

A Pony's Tale

A Pony's Tale
A year in the life of a foal

Photographs by Jane Burton and Kim Taylor
Text by Michael Allaby and Jane Burton

EBURY PRESS LONDON

Published by Ebury Press
Division of The National Magazine Company Ltd
Colquhoun House
27-37 Broadwick Street
London W1V 1FR

First impression 1987

ISBN 0 85223 632 8

AN EDDISON · SADD EDITION
Edited, designed and produced by
Eddison/Sadd Editions Limited
2 Kendall Place, London W1H 3AH

Phototypeset by Bookworm Typesetting,
Manchester, England
Origination by Columbia Offset, Singapore
Printed and bound by Tonsa, San Sebastian, Spain

Contents

THE PARENTS

Porcelain
Champion Keston Porcelain

Fidelity
Supreme Champion Keston Fidelity

THE PONY

Dresden
Pitchwood Dresden

Introduction

I always wanted a pony!

I can remember plaguing my parents to convert the coal-shed into a stable, so that I could keep a pony in it! It might just have held the smallest Shetland. Then came the blitz and the flying bombs; we children were sent away to boarding schools in the country, where I envied those few privileged evacuees whose ponies accompanied them to rural safety. Towards the end of the war I settled down at last, in my fourteenth school, still in the depths of the country. I still longed for my own pony, and rode whenever I could, wonderful long rides through parkland and moors on the edge of Dartmoor, and, in the holidays, more sedate rides in Richmond Park. I must have done enough school work to get me through the exams, but I remember hours spent drawing, modelling, painting, and carving animals of all kinds, especially ponies. The longing for a pony of my own was eventually submerged by other preoccupations, but an abiding interest and love of ponies, indeed of horses of all kinds, has remained.

Now, after many years and with this pony book in prospect, I found myself resurrecting that childhood dream: I would have my own pony at last! For a while I seriously entertained the notion of acquiring an in-foal mare and keeping her here to photograph the birth and the foal's first year. Soon I had offers of several mares, rescue animals in need of a good home as well as mares on loan. But this book was to be about natural pony behaviour. Ponies are herd animals; a mare and her foal are hardly a herd. What about the stallion, and the young stock that form a large part of any natural herd? Our land, thanks to the poor soil and the wild rabbits, provides scarcely enough grazing for our geese, let alone a whole herd of ponies.

So I began to look around for an established herd whose owners would be willing for me to photograph their animals, and was very fortunate to find, at Pitchwood Stud, not far away, the ideal herd: beautiful ponies of all ages in lovely surroundings. There I could come and go as I pleased, and spend all day with the ponies if I wanted. To be allowed to photograph the birth of 'our' foal was a privilege, and following his progress a delight – *almost* as great as if he was actually my own pony!

I hope some of the pleasure and enjoyment that Kim and I had in watching and photographing the foal through his first year is conveyed in the words and pictures of this book.

Jane Burton

Jane Burton
Albury 1987

The beginning

About five thousand years ago, when for the first time a human scrambled on to the back of a startled pony and rode it, in spite of its initial protestations, galloping like the wind, wild and exuberant across the grassy plains, history changed course. A partnership was established between humans and one of the most social of all animal species, earning the pony a very special place in our affections. Probably the event occurred somewhere in the Middle East. Of course, that rider remains anonymous, but we can respond still to his or her courage, spirit and sense of fun.

Many breeds of ponies have been produced since then, and from more than one ancestral wild stock, but physically and psychologically ponies have changed little. Dresden, whose story we are about to tell, was born in the small hours of a cold Monday morning in spring. He will soon learn to accept humans, but the reactions to the world around him that he inherits or learns from Porcelain, his mother, and from the other ponies he will meet are not much different from those of a wild pony.

Porcelain in the foaling box for the night. She puts her head over the door, expecting a titbit. Will she foal down tonight? Three weeks ago it looked as if she would foal early. Now it seems as if she will never foal.

Pregnancy

Diary · Pregnancy

For three weeks we had been sitting up in the stable all night in shifts watching Porcelain. We had been cold and uncomfortable and suffered from lack of sleep. Porcelain had been warm and peaceful, alternately munching her hay or bedding (best barley straw), or dozing, either on her feet or lying down. We learnt all about the nocturnal behaviour of a pregnant mare, and it was very boring! She seemed to have no regular pattern of sleeping and eating.

Porcelain has been dozing couched for an hour. She is about to go into deep sleep. With a sigh she will lay her head down on the straw for flat-out sleep.

As winter gave way to an unpromising spring, Porcelain's pregnancy approached its term. Her foal had been conceived early in May, almost a year ago, for the gestation period for a mare is long. Pregnancy lasts 340 to 350 days, and may be longer still for mares living in the wild.

Wild ponies live in herds. They must move together in search of pasture and at any time the whole herd may need to flee from danger. Until they can run as fast as adults foals are a handicap, but the inconvenience is minimized, for most of them are born in the spring, within a few days of one another. The foals grow and develop together, and the herd is no more hindered by a number of foals than it would be by one.

In all female mammals ovulation is controlled by hormones, but in mares it is the length of daylight that regulates the hormonal system. In March, when the days grow longer than the nights, mares become fertile, and they remain so until the days start drawing in again, in September. Mating can occur at any time during this period, but the stallions' secretion of male hormones is also influenced by day length, and most foals are conceived early in the season. Breeding is coordinated within the herd.

Porcelain eating hay. The steady munching sound has a soporific effect on anyone struggling to stay awake in a stable at night.

Births tend to be synchronized. When the first mare gives birth the smell often excites other pregnant mares and this stimulus makes them secrete the hormones that cause labour to begin. In this way the first birth sets the timing for the remainder, so that foals can be born up to a month early or late.

As her pregnancy advanced, Porcelain grew more placid, although she was suspicious of males and might have reacted with a flash of anger had a stallion approached her. Later she became more tranquil and, as the foal grew inside her, more and more of her time was spent feeding or resting.

She went on feeding right up to the time her foal was due. Had she been living wild, her winter diet would have consisted of the tough leaves of evergreens and old grass, rather than sweet-smelling hay, and even that meagre fare might have been scarce. It would have taken her most of each short day to collect enough, and then she would have had to gather her strength for the birth and produce milk to sustain her infant. Feeding is an urgent, full-time task for any mare.

Porcelain was carrying a single foal, and by the third week in March it could be seen moving inside her. Twin foals sometimes occur, and even triplets are not unknown, but it is unusual for a mare to carry more than one foal at a time, and rare for more than one foal to survive from a multiple birth. Where two or more foals do survive they are likely to be weak. A foal, after all, requires a large amount of food, which its mother must manufacture from a diet that is not very nutritious. If the food has to be shared both foals are likely to suffer.

Diary · Pregnancy

When Porcelain did nothing but doze and munch all night there was the danger that we would be lulled into a false sense of nothing else ever going to happen. Tonight she was unusually restless, kept lying down, getting up again, kicking up at her belly, and pawing the straw. The muscles each side of her tail root seemed to seethe, and the foal was very active too. But the mare's udder had not bagged up any more, nor were her teats waxed up, so it was another false alarm. We kept thinking the waters would surely break any minute. But in the end Porcelain settled down to doze again until daylight dawned, when she went over to the window to watch the roe buck that had crept out of the woods to feed along the paddock hedge. Mares nearly always drop their foals at night, so if nothing had happened by daybreak we could go home. The only result of yet another night's watching was that we could say we had not missed the birth – yet!

The birth

Diary · Birth

At first when we went into the stables tonight Porcelain was dozing with her back to the door. Soon she started moving restlessly round the box, pawing the straw and kicking her belly. We had had that sort of false alarm before, of course. But then she backed herself up against the far wall in her more usual dozing place, and her whole posture was different. Instead of dozing with neck horizontal and head down, her neck was arched and her head up. She looked slightly tense, with jaw muscles tight, nostrils a little flared. She was sweating slightly. I could not see it from outside the box, but her teats had waxed up. Although no outward sign of contractions showed, her belly had dropped into a keel. Surely tonight would be the night. She *must* be going to foal down tonight.

Tail raised, Porcelain prepares to give birth. The foetal sac has appeared, and Porcelain paces around the box, lies down, and gets up again, as the contractions become stronger.

It is not easy to tell when a mare is about to foal. Her udders fill and swell several days before the event. When her foal was due Porcelain was moved into a foaling box in preparation. She was restless, moving about the box and pawing at her bedding, then shifting her weight from one foot to another. Sometimes she would lie down to sleep, breathing noisily, moving her legs as she dreamed, and leaping to her feet the moment she woke, as though startled. At other times she would doze for a while, on her feet, only to start moving again the moment she awoke, looking at her flank, swishing her tail. All these are signs that labour is about to begin, but they can continue for a long time and false alarms are common. Porcelain kept them up for more than three weeks.

Giving birth is a very private matter for a mare. She prefers to be alone and can hold back her foal, for hours if necessary, if she feels insecure. Porcelain was confined, but a wild mare will move away from the herd to some secluded spot. For reasons no one understands, some mares choose wet ground or even a pond or ditch, and foals can be drowned by being born directly into water.

If a foal expected in the evening has not been born by dawn, the birth is unlikely to take place until the following night. Wild or domesticated, almost all foals are born at night.

Porcelain became even more restless. Her teats had now

developed waxy plugs, a sure sign the birth was imminent. She kicked at her belly with her hind feet and the muscles near the root of her tail were twitching. Her face muscles grew tense, and she began to sweat a little. She lay down from time to time, dozing between contractions, and even fell into a deep sleep with her eyes wide open and staring. Her belly altered its shape, making a keel like the bottom of a boat. The foal is contained within a membranous sac filled with fluid. As the powerful muscles of the uterus start their rhythmic contractions the sac is propelled into the birth canal with the fluid ahead of the foal, forming a soft, flexible mass, like a cushion, opening the way and emerging first. Before the foal is born the emerging sac bursts, releasing all its fluid, the 'waters'.

At this point the mare usually lies down, as Porcelain did, and she may lick at the waters, and 'flehm', an action many animals perform, but not humans. The mare sniffs the fluid with a deep intake of breath, raises her head, and rolls back her upper lip. This partly seals her nose and traps a small amount of air containing molecules of the odour which dissolve in nasal secretions and are passed for analysis to the Jacobson's organ, a recess just above the soft palate inside her nose, rich in nerve endings.

The birth itself immediately follows the breaking of the waters, and it is quick. In a normal birth the front feet of the foal emerge first and the infant, partly shrouded in the membrane in which it has lived until now, is born, sometimes in as little as five minutes, rarely in more than forty-five. Porcelain took ten minutes to give birth to her foal. While she is giving birth a mare is separated from her herd, helpless, exposed despite her choice of a secluded place, and vulnerable to attack by predators. She cannot afford to devote long to the task. Many an anxious or admiring human watcher has missed the birth by disappearing at the wrong moment to make a cup of coffee.

While it lay in the womb the foal was nourished from the placenta, to which it remains attached by its umbilical cord until the mother breaks it. With further contractions, the placenta follows the birth, sometimes after an interval of an hour or more. The mare will lick it, flehm at it and nibble it. Some mares may go further and try to eat it. There is a real danger of choking if a mare attempts to swallow a placenta and to avoid this it should be removed altogether as soon as the mother has had a chance to examine it.

The mare sniffs her foal and gives a quiet, gentle nicker to which the foal responds, moving clumsily in her direction as it does so, and as she pulls away the membranes and licks the foal the first bond is formed between the mother and her offspring. Her gentle call and licking attract the foal but they also stimulate it to start moving, stretching its limbs, searching, and breathing more deeply, in fact to start living.

Diary · Birth

Shortly after the bag appeared, Porcelain lay down again, then got up and, as she did so, there was a great cascade as the waters burst. Soon after, the forefeet of the foal appeared. Porcelain went down with her quarters inconveniently into a corner of the box. She got up again, churned around, and flung herself down in another corner. Human hands helped by pulling on the foal's feet in time with the mare's contractions, to get its shoulders past her pelvis and save her becoming exhausted with the effort. Once the shoulders are through, a foal slides out comparatively easily. With a sudden whoosh Porcelain's foal was right out and lying in the straw.

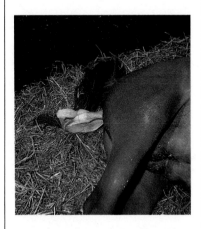

The forefeet of the foal, still within the foetal membranes; a foal is normally born head first. Porcelain has gone down in a corner of the foaling box for the final labour. Her udder is bagged up ready for the hungry foal's first feed.

13

A new foal

As the foal was born, the membranes came away from its head, and it lay at Porcelain's tail partially covered by the caul, very wet and still attached to the umbilical cord. Porcelain appeared delighted with it, sniffed its nose and nickered a tender little greeting. She remained lying down for some time, recovering her strength.

While they both wait for the placenta to come away, Porcelain bends her head right round to sniff the newborn foal's nose.

Wet and bedraggled, but fully formed and healthy, a colt (male) foal, had been born. As Porcelain lay on her side, recovering from the birth, he lay beside her, the right way up, head raised, and with his legs folded beneath him. The humans called him Dresden.

Finally Porcelain rolled over from her side and stood up again, her movement pulling away the membranes, the 'caul', from the rear of his body and freeing his limbs completely. The umbilical cord was broken at the same time. The blood vessels in Dresden's abdomen sealed themselves in advance of the break, preventing any bleeding. She turned, sniffed at his nose, and then began to lick him dry.

The initial nose-to-nose contact between a mare and her foal serves several purposes, but it is first and foremost a gentle, careful greeting and enquiry, and the foal responds as a junior to a senior member of the herd. He lowers his head and ears, bares his toothless gums, and at the same time snaps his jaws with a movement much like the one he will use when suckling, making a similar sound. At this stage the foal is not to know which large

14

As Porcelain walks away, the membranes are pulled away from the foal and the umbilical cord broken naturally with the minimum of bleeding.

objects he should treat with respect and which he can safely ignore, so he is often confused. He will give his 'mouthing' response to almost anything large that moves, probably in the hope that it will placate an aggressor. A human may illicit it, or even a machine. As he grows older he gives the 'mouthing' response more rarely. By the time he is fully mature, the foal will abandon it altogether.

Dresden had started breathing of his own accord as soon as the front part of his body was clear of his mother's pelvis and he could move his chest, but Porcelain now licked his muzzle, clearing the nostrils and stimulating him to breathe more deeply. The muzzle is the part of a pony's body that is most highly sensitive to touch and Porcelain's attention to his muzzle also made Dresden curl his tongue and make his first sucking movements. Like all young mammals, foals are born hungry.

The close examination with which Porcelain accompanied the licking involved a thorough sniffing. Little is known about the keenness of a pony's sense of smell, although in arid places ponies are known to use it to find their way to water over long distances. They can also detect other animals by smell, sometimes using a path they cannot see to cross difficult terrain by following the scent of the animals, often sheep, that made it. Ponies also rely on their sense of smell socially, among themselves. Every individual has a characteristic personal smell. Porcelain familiarized herself with the smell of Dresden, and memorized it. In the days and weeks to come she would need it, for it is by smell rather than their appearance or voice that mares, like ewes and most other animals of the open grasslands, recognize their own offspring.

Diary · Birth

While mare and foal lay quietly, the foal's umbilical cord closed in preparation for the break. (If the cord is severed too soon, a foal can bleed to death.) After about half an hour Porcelain scrambled to her feet, breaking the cord and passing the placenta. Her moving away pulled the membranes right off the foal. She turned to smell the afterbirth, licked and nibbled at it, but was prevented from trying to eat it because of the very real danger that she might choke on it. The foal remained lying where it was born. To keep it warm and cushion its efforts to stand, fresh dry straw was heaped all round it. The afterbirth was removed for later inspection by a vet, to be sure that the complete placenta had been passed; and gentian violet wound dressing was sprayed on the foal's cord to prevent any infection developing.

First steps

Diary · First hours

Porcelain licked and nibbled at the wet foal, while he made his first efforts to get to his feet. His hind legs started to go in one direction, his front legs in the other. Lying there surrounded by legs he looked rather like a giant octopus. As his efforts grew stronger he would almost get up, but then stagger, overbalance and fling himself on to his back. The nudgings of his mother really didn't help him at all. He would just be almost on his feet when her nosing would send him toppling over again.

Porcelain licking the foal's wet coat as he struggles to stand. She is so delighted with her new foal she cannot leave him alone to let him find his feet in peace.

When the young have been born and mares have rejoined the herd with their new foals, the youngsters begin to explore their surroundings, race around, and then return to their mothers to feed. At first the foals will not recognize their mothers, and each mare must be able to distinguish her own foal from all the others.

Dresden was small and weak, but wide awake, his eyes and ears open. He could see, hear and smell, and his body and its senses had to be pressed into service immediately. Unlike a kitten or puppy, from the moment he was born his body took over the task of regulating its own temperature. His mother did not have to keep him warm. He was born very nearly ready for action. All he needed was a little practice and he would be able to use his body to move as freely as its size would permit.

Those hoofed animals that live in herds in open country depend for their safety on keeping together and on the move. They have no other means of self-defence. A pony can kick, but this will avail it little against a determined predator, and it can bite, but its teeth are designed for crushing, not piercing or cutting. Hoofs and blunt teeth are no match for sharp teeth and claws, and it has no way of protecting its back. If a mare is vulnerable while she gives birth, a helpless, immobile foal is even more so.

Small and weak though he was, Dresden could not afford to remain helpless and immobile for long. Within minutes he was struggling to stand, trying to draw his feet beneath his body and keep them there long enough to raise himself. His mother kept

nudging him with her muzzle, but if this was meant to help him it was misguided because she kept pushing him the wrong way, so he overbalanced.

It is vital for a mare to recognize her own foal close to, so she studies his personal scent carefully.

His legs were fully formed, but they were long in relation to the size of his body, most of their length being in the lower part, below the 'knees' and 'elbows', so they looked slightly ungainly, and the main muscles were concentrated higher up, near the 'hips' and 'shoulders'. The length of his limbs gave him a long stride, which would help him keep up with the other ponies when the herd moved, but they were controlled by muscles and a nervous system that were being pressed into service for the first time, and these were difficult to master. The spindly legs splayed in all directions, moving independently when they should have worked in unison, sometimes even toppling him on to his back. His efforts were complicated by the confined space of the foaling

17

Diary · First hours

Soon the foal was beginning to feel really hungry. He made a sucking mouth with grooved tongue sticking out. The urgent need to suck made him increase his efforts to stand.

The foal's feet slip out in every direction as he makes valiant efforts to stand up.

box. Had he been born in the open, like a wild foal, he would have had ample room to manoeuvre. As it was, he crashed repeatedly into the wooden walls and his human friends had to help him.

He persevered. Since he had never experienced it before, he could not recognize hunger as such, but felt it as increasing discomfort in his stomach. It drove him to intensify his struggles, until at last the technique was mastered and he was standing by himself. He was then about one hour old.

That done, his next task was to find food. He had a general idea of where to look, being attracted to anything that moved or gave a nicker. For the foal born in a secluded place away from the herd the only large moving or vocal object is its mother, so the attraction is sensible, but if there are several moving objects nearby the foal will choose the largest. As it was, Dresden moved

first towards a human, and had to be gently redirected.

He knew the kind of place he was supposed to find and set about looking for two columns with a dark recess between them, ignoring everything else. Sometimes foals have to be bottle-fed and it can be very difficult to interest them in the bottle unless it is presented in the correct kind of location. Usually it is, because a human offering a bottle to a foal tends naturally to adopt a posture the foal can recognize, standing upright but leaning forward a little, with the feet apart, presenting the bottle at about waist height.

At first Dresden made mistakes. This was only to be expected, for his impulses were somewhat vague, he did not know what reward to expect, and everything around him was unfamiliar. The corner between two walls of the foaling box attracted him, but it proved unsatisfactory and he abandoned it. He approached Porcelain from the wrong end and rummaged briefly and hopelessly at her chest. He was Porcelain's second foal, so she knew what was supposed to happen and could help him. She turned to present her side to his probing head and moved a hind leg back a little to allow him better access to her udder. Even if he had known what a teat looked or smelled like finding it would still have presented problems for him because it was hidden below his line of sight and to reach it he had to stoop and bend his head upwards at the same time.

Diary · First hours

As he struggled to stand up, the foal overbalanced several times and sent himself crashing quite violently against the walls of the loosebox. To prevent him bruising himself he was held upright for a while until he got the hang of keeping his legs more or less underneath him. A little less tottery, he was released, but then tried to follow the human support instead of his mother. But hunger drove him to transfer his attentions back to Porcelain. He was all legs and head, with the centre of gravity over the shoulders, so any movement forward resulted in an unsteady sort of rocking-horse canter.

The foal is on his feet, but wobbly. Porcelain continues to lick and nudge him, which hardly helps his balancing act. His coat is, by this time, getting fairly dry.

A bond is formed

Diary · First hours

The first sucks that the foal managed were surprisingly short, but obviously enough to give him his first intake of the vital colostrum. He licked his lips and savoured the taste of the fluid after each suck. Not long after that first feed he passed the meconium, and then his first stale (urine). Porcelain was very interested in both events, as we were also. We could now be assured that all was well with the foal: he had eaten and he had dunged. All systems were seen to be working, and we could pack up now and go home to bed.

At last the foal has found the correct corner. He makes a sucking mouth in anticipation as he reaches up towards a teat.

It can be a testing time for a foal. Most mares try to help their infants find the place to suckle, turning themselves and pushing the foal in the right direction, but it is not unknown for a mare to reject her foal or even attack it, although this has never been seen in the wild. All ponies that live in a herd are familiar with foals because they are around all the time, and very young ones will often approach a mare who is not their mother. A domesticated mare may not have this experience and may never have met a foal until she has one herself. When that happens she may find this small, strange, insistent animal alarming and try to rid herself of it.

It took him about an hour, but in the end Dresden found a teat by a mixture of luck, judgement, and help from his mother. He nudged it, a little milk was released and some of it fell on his nose; he licked it away, liked the taste, licked the teat, and his licking stimulated the flow. If the mare has not yet expelled the placenta this stimulus will also start more uterine contractions that will make her do so. More or less by accident Porcelain's rather small teat found its way into Dresden's mouth and that stimulated him to suck strongly. All healthy young mammals know how to suck.

The first milk that all young mammals receive, and which a foal drinks until it is a few days old, is called 'colostrum' and it differs chemically from the milk produced later. It is richer in

proteins and contains antibodies that confer protection on the infant against all the infections to which the mother has been exposed and therefore is immune, including, of course, those immunities she acquired from the colostrum she received from her own mother. A foal that misses its colostrum may be unusually susceptible to the many illnesses it encounters when it moves more freely in the outside world.

Young as he was, Dresden was learning fast. The milk tasted good and the discomfort disappeared from his stomach. The foal remembers with pleasure this first experience of food and wants to repeat it. At first it will suck at anything that looks even approximately like a dark recess between two upright columns, but will give up when no milk is forthcoming. It will approach other large animals of the wrong species, and other adults of its own, only to be turned away, learning quickly that only its own mother will accept and satisfy it. Before long its innate impulse to suck and need to feed are refined by trial and error to a precise relationship with its mother, whom it will follow anywhere without hesitation. Dresden was now about two hours old. He could see, hear and smell. He could stand and walk, at least for a short distance. He had found a teat and started to suckle. The intimate relationship between foal and mare was established, and next time Dresden would find and identify Porcelain more easily, and she him. It had been a busy couple of hours.

The foal lifts his tail and bends his hind legs as he passes the meconium or first dung. Porcelain watches, before smelling the black mess intently.

Diary · First hours

After three weeks of waiting up night after night we were rewarded by actually being there when the foal was born – we had not missed the birth, in spite of all those gloomy predictions from other pony watchers! The birth itself was very quick, probably about ten minutes from the first appearance of the sac to the foal being right out. He probably took around an hour to struggle on to his feet, and then another hour actually to find the teat. We drove home through the freezing mist long before dawn, elated that the long vigil had not been in vain.

'Ours' was the second foal born this year at Pitchwood Stud – Pitchwood Dresden (stable name Dizzie) out of Keston Porcelain. First to arrive had been Pitchwood Vivaldi (stable name Whisky) out of Buriwest Brandy Snap (Brandy), born some two months before. A week later two more foals arrived on the same night: Pitchwood Celebration (stable name Millie), a really delightful little foal, more like a roe fawn than a pony, out of Waterman's Filumena (Mena); and Pitchwood Royal Salute (Percy) born just before dawn on the Queen's birthday. He was another chestnut, like Dresden, but bigger and with a star instead of a blaze. His mother was the old boss mare Rotherwood Peepshine. One other foal was due, but not for another month or so. All but Millie were by Pitchwood Stud's Supreme Champion stallion Keston Fidelity (better known as Fizz).

Up until the time of its birth, a mammal is nourished from the placenta, by food supplied from the bloodstream of its mother. It does not eat in the usual sense. This does not mean, however, that it is born with its digestive tract completely empty. Its bowel contains 'meconium', a mixture of substances secreted into the gut from glands nearby and fluid it swallowed in the final stages of its development; its bladder also contains the by-products of this fluid. As he searched for a teat and his first meal Dresden urinated and rid himself of his meconium.

Porcelain sniffed and licked at the meconium while Dresden was passing it. Urine and dung, even the first to be passed by a newborn foal, have a smell characteristic of the individual whose body produced them. Ponies are not territorial, but they do use dung and urine to make scent marks. The smell will tell a pony the sex of the animal that left it and in some cases it may even reveal that pony's identity. When she sniffed and tasted the meconium Porcelain was sampling and memorizing Dresden's personal smell. It reinforced the bond between mother and infant.

During the night Dresden was born, three other pregnant mares lay in nearby foaling boxes. Had they been members of a wild herd, all three might have given birth to their foals.

As he moved around the box looking for his first meal, Dresden was using his legs. He was walking, clumsily and unreliably at first, but then more confidently. No-one had to teach him what he was supposed to do with his legs, but he had to learn for himself how to control them and move without falling. Humans, who walk on two legs, may think four legs makes walking much easier. In some ways it does, but it also means twice the number of limbs to control. The trick is to keep three feet on the ground at all times and to keep the centre of gravity inside the triangle made by those three feet. If the centre of gravity moves outside the triangle the animal is off-balance and may fall. So Dresden walked, and all ponies walk, with his front and hind legs one quarter of a cycle out of step, right forefoot, left hind, left forefoot, right hind.

His progress was rapid, but still more was required of him. Had they been living in the open, Porcelain would have started moving by now, drifting unhurriedly back towards the herd, grazing here and there as she went, and Dresden would have had to remain close to her side, following wherever she led, and probably stopping her now and then when he remembered the pleasure to be had from suckling.

Walking would have been enough to keep him beside her, but the slightest alarm would have made Porcelain increase her pace, and Dresden would have had to move faster, too. She would not travel so fast as to leave him behind, no matter how grave the danger, but because he was so much smaller than his mother, even a brisk walk for her would mean he had to canter.

This is not simply a matter of walking faster. The limbs are moved in the same sequence, but there is a moment of suspension during each stride; landing first on the right hind foot, the right fore and left hind strike the ground almost simultaneously, followed by the left forefoot. At a canter he could probably travel at around 10 miles an hour (16 km/h). It would not be fast enough to escape being run down by a predator, but it might get him into the centre of the herd quickly, where he would be hidden.

When a wild herd is threatened the foals move to the centre. A predator might find it easier to capture a foal than an adult, but even a pack of wolves would be satisfied with just one victim.

Now dry and almost steady on his long legs, the foal takes another suck. Porcelain, still entranced with her new baby, repeatedly checks his smell.

Growing up

When Dresden was no more than a few hours old he could walk beside his mother, and keep up with her provided she did not move too fast. Had they been living in the wild, Porcelain would have rejoined the herd as soon as she had rested after giving birth, and Dresden would have gone with her.

A foal remains a helpless infant for only a very short time, but this is no disadvantage. It allows much longer for the youngster to play actively, by itself or with others of its own age.

By the time he is two weeks old, the age at which a kitten would be starting to open its eyes, Dresden is playing outdoors and has begun to explore the exciting world around him. By six weeks, when kittens are still playing in and around the nest and have not yet completely mastered their limbs, he will be meeting other ponies, playing with other foals, and learning how to behave as a new member of the pony herd, which is one of the most highly organized of all animal societies.

With ostentatious trot and tail raised like a flag, Porcelain leads Dresden away: he has gone near another mare and foal, and been kicked in the ribs. Now, whenever he seems to be venturing too close again, Porcelain rounds him away to the far end of the paddock.

Exploring and learning

This spring has been the coldest and wettest on record. Trees are scarcely greening yet, the grass is poor. It has been too cold to put the mares and foals out until now, but today was a bit milder so they were out in the nursery paddock for a few hours.

Porcelain eagerly crops her first grass for more than ten days, while Dresden investigates his new world. Here he is smelling the rainwater in a deep hoof print and has to bend his front legs to get his nose down below grass level.

Exploration in the new world of grass, hedges and trees was as nearly a full-time occupation as a young foal could manage. Like all very young mammals, Dresden was asleep for a good deal of the time and he needed to feed up to four times every hour. There was not time to wander far from Porcelain between meals and she stayed nearby during his naps.

His most important and useful exploratory equipment were his nose and tongue. He sniffed everything and tasted most things, but before he could do either there was another technique he had to learn. His legs were so long and his neck so short that when he stood upright he was unable to reach the ground with his mouth. Adults can do this, but it did not work when Dresden tried it. He had to spread his forelegs wide apart and bend them in order to lower the front part of his body or, better still and certainly more restful, he had to lie down. Once he had solved the problem a whole universe of smells and

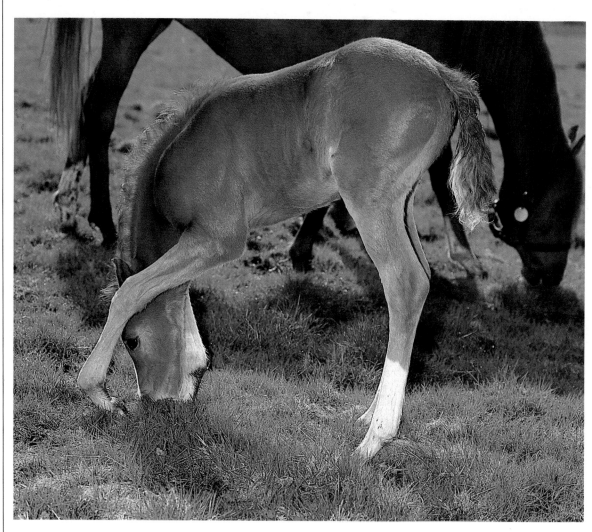

flavours was displayed before him.

He sniffed at puddles of rainwater caught in depressions made by the hoofs of other ponies, and he tried drinking. Ponies do not lap at liquids in the way that cats and dogs do. They pucker their lips together and suck. This allows them to drink water without disturbing it too much, and they can take the clear water from near the surface of a muddy pool or ditch without stirring up mud from the bottom. It is a sucking action, but not the same as suckling, and Dresden had to practise before he could do it properly.

The grass and other herbs on which Porcelain grazed were starting to be of great interest to him. He was born without teeth, but now his first 'milk' teeth had erupted. He had two incisors and three premolars in each jaw and from the moment they appeared he began to use them. He was able to nibble at the pasture but he could not really eat much of it. He had no molars

Diary · Eleven days

When Porcelain was led out from the stables Dresden followed close at her heels. This was the very first time he had ever been outside a loosebox. He knew what his mother looked like and smelled like from close to, so followed her closely at first. But the sight of grass and trees and the big wide world amazed him, so he stood and stared about him. Suddenly he needed his mother. Help, where was she? Porcelain, still being led, was halfway down the paddock, stepping out eagerly. Dresden could see her, he wasn't short-sighted. But he was unable to recognize her. She had six legs and a quite different-shaped front end. He panicked, running about blindly and whinnying with fear at being all alone. Porcelain had to be led back to allow him to see her at close quarters again before he would calm down and follow her to the next paddock where they could be turned out for the day.

As soon as she was released Porcelain put her head down and hardly looked up until it was time to go back to the stable for the night. She could watch her foal all the time as she grazed. He was not into grass-eating yet, so he had plenty of time for investigating.

Experimentally he smelled and tasted old dung, dead leaves, twigs, and earth, but spat them out again. Clenching his jaws on a tuft of grass at the same time as he tried to run, he nearly went head over heels.

Giraffe-like, Dresden spreads his front feet wide apart so that his mouth can reach the ground. He is eating earth.

Diary · Twelve days

Dresden liked the old manure heap in the corner of the paddock. He liked the very bright green grass to taste. He also thought he would like the young nettles, but they stung his mouth. He backed away, lips curled, and rubbed his muzzle on his forelegs to ease the tingling. He seemed to think it fun to get bogged down in black muck. The effort of freeing his feet would send him off on another scampering bout.

Like a little racehorse Dresden runs flat out, galloping in a short burst away from Porcelain. He will bounce to a halt, wheel as if startled, and rush back to her again.

with which to crush and grind such tough material, and his body could not digest it. His experiments helped him to distinguish between plants that were painful to touch, that stung or pricked his sensitive lips and nose, and those that felt more gentle, that soon he would come to regard as edible.

He did sample fresh dung, however, dropped by other ponies, and some of this he swallowed. It contained partly digested food together with large numbers of bacteria. These bacteria live in the digestive tracts of ponies and break down the cellulose from which the walls of plant cells are made. They make it possible for a pony to digest its food and Dresden needed them. They would live inside him, multiply, and be ready and waiting for the day when Dresden sent his first proper meal of grass down to them.

He was now fully mobile and enjoyed galloping around the field. Having mastered the walk and canter, Dresden had to learn two new sequences of steps, the trot and the gallop. In order to trot he had to move two legs in unison, right forefoot and left hind, then left forefoot and right hind, adjusting his balance all the time, but by moving quickly each pair of legs caught him as he began to topple towards them. The gallop, for moving at full speed, is almost a leap but not quite, because the hoofs reach the ground one at a time – right hind, left hind, right forefoot, left forefoot. As the front hoofs leave the ground the hind legs are swung forward level with them or slightly in front so as to cover as much distance as possible before striking the ground and launching on to the next stride.

Galloping gave him exercise to strengthen his muscles and

improve his coordination. Apart from that he enjoyed it. Yet it had a serious purpose. As soon as he could gallop the entire herd was safer. If the other ponies had to run he could run with them. He could not move as fast as an adult at full speed because he was smaller and had a shorter stride, but provided there was warning of an impending attack from predators he would have been able to keep up as the herd moved out of range, at less than full speed. Porcelain would not have had to trail behind to protect him and the herd would not have been weakened by her absence.

It had not taken him long to gain the confidence needed to move away from her side. Every animal has around it a small area of 'personal space'. If another animal enters this space without invitation or the proper signals of greeting, the invasion will seem threatening and the threatened individual will move away or return the threat. While he remained very close to her Dresden was inside Porcelain's space, safe because as long as he was so close she would protect him as she would protect herself. When he moved away from her he was alone, inside his own space and it was small, strange, and he did not know how to defend it. It was a big step towards independence, and when no threat appeared he began to feel braver and moved just a little further. The world was not a dangerous place after all. It was somewhere to run, play, and investigate fearlessly, so long as mother was not too far away. He was suspicious of large and possibly threatening animals but apart from those he had no real sense of danger.

Dresden running in dizzy circles round his mother. Sometimes he gives a fair imitation of a really mean bucking bronco, but here he is returning at a more leisurely canter.

Diary · Twelve days

Dresden's running never took him far from his mother. If he seemed to be venturing too far she called him, and he would come racing back again. After a little of this high-speed exercise he would have to stop to get his breath back. He also needed to refuel frequently, but soon found drinking and panting at the same time was not a practical proposition.

Diary · Twelve days

Foals whizz in circles round their mothers for only the first two to three weeks. We were already more than halfway through that period with Dresden.

Dresden had learnt his lesson about nettles! Today he sniffed them but kept his nose well out. His preoccupation at present was with fresh dung. Three cows and a calf now shared the paddock, and Dresden sniffed long and noisily at some cowpats, and deliberately put his forefeet in them. He also picked up and played about with fresh dung; he spat much of it out, but may also have swallowed some. He also actually ate some grass, for the first time. He was scouring a bit, and had messy quarters, but this was not from eating his first greens. Porcelain had just come to the end of her foaling heat; changes in the hormones in her milk had led to Dresden scouring, and it was quite normal.

Dresden taking off on another high-speed tour. He may never again put as much voluntary effort into running as he now puts into these exuberant bouts.

Playing

All was well so long as Dresden and Porcelain were within sight of one another. Porcelain would keep an eye on him, let him play by himself, and call him back only if he strayed too far or towards danger. Were Dresden to find himself alone, separated from his mother, he would cry in distress, with a pathetic squeak, and Porcelain would hear him. Ponies are very vocal, have very keen hearing, and the distress cry is the first call a foal is likely to use. It brings an immediate response. Porcelain also had a cry, a nicker that would summon Dresden, and which he was supposed to obey instantly.

From a distance Dresden could not tell Porcelain from any other adult, and he identified other ponies by their general shape. If anything altered the shape, such as a human leading or standing very close to a pony, he might ignore the strange object and go on searching for something more familiar. Had there been a group of adults he would have gone to the nearest. If he approached the wrong individual he would be sniffed and sent away with enough of a threat to make him retreat rapidly, mouthing his submission, try someone else and go on trying until he found his mother.

Most adult ponies are very tolerant of foals, and mothers are especially tolerant of their own young. They allow themselves to be butted, climbed over, pawed and generally abused with gentle good humour.

Diary · Fifteen days

A warm sunny spring-like morning at last – not just the odd patch of sun between showers! Dresden was feeling particularly playful today. Porcelain simply wanted to be left alone to get on with eating grass, but her foal wanted a game.

Opposite *Dresden prancing around Porcelain's head distracts her from grazing. He rears and pretends to bite. His mother bears his antics patiently.*

Left *Now Dresden plays mounting games as if trying to climb his mother's neck. She is not amused, but would never kick her own foal however much he teased her.*

33

Scratching and rolling

Today Dresden found out about another plant that bites – thistles! He stuck his nose into the middle of a large rosette of the prickly leaves, and again had to rub his mouth and lips on his forelegs to take away the soreness. He rubbed on Porcelain's hocks, too.

Dresden had not been running and playing for long before a new need presented itself. He itched, and the only sensible thing to do with an itch is to scratch it. Like all animals, ponies attract lice, ticks and other skin parasites, although a domesticated pony will have human friends to help deal with them. These are not the only cause of minor irritations, however. Bits of mud, burrs, and scratches from thorns all call for attention, and skin and hair need regular maintenance. Ignore a small scratch or cut and it may become infected and turn into something much more serious.

No animal has to learn that scratching brings comfort, but some of the more advanced scratching techniques call for a degree of skill. Dresden had incisor teeth, which in most mammals are the basic tools for the job, and his neck and back were flexible. He could reach much of his body and nibble away the itches easily and very happily.

This was splendid, as far as it went. The trouble was that no animal can use its mouth to scratch its own head. This called for

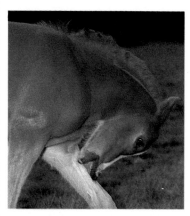

Rubbing his gums on his leg to ease the tingling of the thistle prickles. Two newly erupted upper teeth are revealed as Dresden rubs.

Right *Dresden contorts himself as he reaches round to scratch his own back, gnawing the itch with tiny peg-like incisors.*

a different approach, and some skill. He had to use a foot if he was to reach the area around his ears. This meant balancing on three legs while one hind leg was raised, and remaining in this position long enough and steadily enough to complete the scratch. At the same time he had to bend his head down and to one side to meet the raised foot, so the weight of his head moved to the side that had only one foot on the ground and he had to lean his body far enough the other way to avoid overbalancing. Then he had to judge the pressure and amount of movement needed to deal with the itch. If he scratched too lightly he might make the itch worse. If he scratched too roughly he might hurt himself. His foot, after all, was a hoof.

Foals should not wear collars for fear they might catch a hoof while scratching in this way, and injure themselves trying to struggle free. The warning applies only to foals, for usually it is only foals that use their feet to scratch their heads.

As he grew older, Dresden would use a different technique. He would roll on his back, writhing deliciously until every bit of his

Diary · Fifteen days

Dresden's explorations also extended above ground level to as high up the trunk of an oak tree as he could reach with his mouth, and paw at with a forefoot. The foal was becoming increasingly confident, agile and well balanced, capable of precise small operations as well as sudden bursts of helter-skelter speed.

No doubt Dresden clonked himself painfully a few times before perfecting the delicate eyebrow scratch he performs here. Considering the power in his leg muscles and his extreme youth, such control is amazing.

Diary · Fifteen days

Both Porcelain and Dresden rolled several times in the paddock today. Dresden thought it a great game when his mother went belly-side up and flung her feet about. He whizzed around her excitedly and climbed on her as she heaved to her feet. The first time the foal tried to roll it was hardly a roll at all, not even on to his back. The next was a better try, though he still couldn't roll right over. The third go was a proper roll, over and back several times. After, he leapt lightly to his feet; a little light foal can jump nimbly up, whereas heavy adults often have quite a struggle.

Far left *Dresden lies down close to Porcelain's heels. She walks on, grazing, leaving space for Dresden to roll* below. *After two or three quick rolls with his legs waving, he leaps nimbly to his feet* left.

back, sides, neck and head had been rubbed hard, then stand up and shake vigorously, sending out a shower of dust, sand, and fragments of vegetation.

He was rolling by the time he was two weeks old, though more for fun than to have a serious scratch. First he had to lie down, which he could do already, of course, because he lay down to sleep. He began by bending his forelegs, then his hind legs, so he went down front end first. From there it was not too difficult for him to push himself on to his back and squirm and roll from side to side. An adult pony, intent on scratching, would stay on one side until it was completely comfortable, but if it were elderly and its joints rather stiff, it might not be able to balance on its back and then roll over to the other side. It would have to roll on one side, stand up, then turn around and lie down again to roll the other way.

Returning to an upright position, with his legs beneath his body, Dresden stood up by pushing first with his forelegs. When they were more or less straight he gave a strong heave to straighten his hind legs. It takes considerable strength for a pony to throw its weight forward in this way. Dresden was young, light and agile, but elderly ponies sometimes have difficulty in rising from a lying position.

Ponies lie down and stand up again front end first. Cattle, deer and other large animals do so the other way round, rear end first, pushing up with their hind legs.

37

Sleeping

This must have been the sunniest morning so far this spring; it didn't cloud up until nearly midday. I had followed Dresden around for three hours. As usual he took no notice of me unless I tried to touch him. For my part, I was glad he was not too friendly; a foal forever wanting to put its nose in the camera would have been nothing but a trial!

All the excitement and running around, and the new sights and sounds of the morning finally tired Dresden out and he lay down for a sleep just as the clouds rolled up. For a while he nibbled grass, now easier to reach than when he was standing. Gently he dozed off with his nose resting on the ground, but gradually his head lolled to one side. Occasionally he jerked himself upright and awoke again as if resisting sleep, but finally he laid his head on the grass, and stretched his legs out as he fell asleep. Porcelain just went on grazing round him. No doubt her steady munching lulled him to sleep as it had lulled us in the stable when we had been trying to stay awake!

Dresden still spent a good deal of his time asleep, but like any other mammal he would sleep less as he grew older. Adult ponies need less sleep than most humans. Five hours is enough for most of them, although some sleep rather more, and they sleep in short spells rather than a single long bout, more at night than during the day because at night it is more difficult to move around and graze.

When he felt tired he would almost always lie down and sleep either stretched out on his side or on his front, with his legs tucked beneath him. Sometimes he would bend his head forward, pull back his lips, and balance the weight of his head on his teeth. This rested his neck muscles without bruising his lips.

The skeleton of a pony allows it to sleep while standing without losing its balance, or to lie. Ponies are able to doze standing up, but they usually lie down when they want to sleep deeply.

When a pony sleeps, standing or lying, a part of its brain remains aware of its surroundings. Some animals sleep more deeply than others, and ponies are light sleepers, but their alertness is selective. Other ponies may be moving nearby, rabbits or other small animals may be feeding close to them, and familiar sounds of sheep, cattle, or traffic will reach them, but none of this will disturb them, any more than familiar sounds disturb a human sleeper. If there were a strange sound they would be awake at once, aroused much faster than a human, on their feet and ready to flee. There are predators that hunt by night and in open country ponies have no safe refuge in which to hide. Their enemies find them good to eat, they are unarmed, and they cannot afford the luxury of complete insensibility.

A pony must regard a human as something of an enigma. It ought to be a predator but in practice it rarely kills or even harms ponies. This might be because people move slowly and are fairly easy to evade. So, from the animal's point of view, although humans might like to kill ponies they are unable to do so. But, of course, some humans are familiar and friendly. It is a puzzle, but no pony dares to take chances. When humans are around it must be on its feet and ready to make a run for it should the need arise. The approach of a human will always alert a sleeping pony and by the time the human is close to it the animal will be on its feet. This accounts for the old belief that ponies always sleep standing. They do not, but it is unusual for a human to come across one lying down and asleep.

Most scientists believe that ponies dream, but only while they are lying down. Adults may spend about one-quarter of each sleep period dreaming, but a young foal may dream for almost all the time it is asleep. How can the scientists be so certain? When humans sleep they spend some of the time in 'quiet sleep', when the electrical activity of the brain is quite different from that of a waking person, but at other times brain activity is much more like that of a person who is awake. This is 'active sleep' and if you wake a person during a period of active sleep they will usually say they had been dreaming. Other mammals, including ponies, show similar patterns of brain activity, so it seems reasonable to suppose that they, too, are dreaming during their active sleep periods.

If ponies dream, do they have bad dreams – nightmares? Certainly they can sleep restlessly and noisily. A sleeping foal may make sucking movements and sounds and all ponies are likely to scratch themselves, move their legs, make nickering sounds that might be suppressed neighs, and some of them snore very loudly indeed.

Dresden stretches out in deep sleep, peaceful and secure in the knowledge that his mother is always grazing nearby.

Meeting other ponies

Diary · Fifteen days

Porcelain and Dresden shared their nursery paddock with Brandy and her foal Whisky. Whisky was quite a bit bigger and more advanced than Dresden. In fact Whisky was at the stage of wanting to play with a friend of his own age, although neither mares were ready to allow this yet, and would threaten the other's foal if it came too near their own. Their paddock was not very large, but there was room enough for both mares to keep out of each other's way. However, it was not large enough for more than the two pairs; had another mare and foal been introduced, there would have been constant chivvying as each sought to maintain her private space. So to prevent bickering, the other two Pitchwood mares that had also foaled were put out into another similar-sized paddock next to Dresden's: Peepshine with Percy and Filumena with Millie. Dresden would watch them from a safe distance and the mares all grazed in peace.

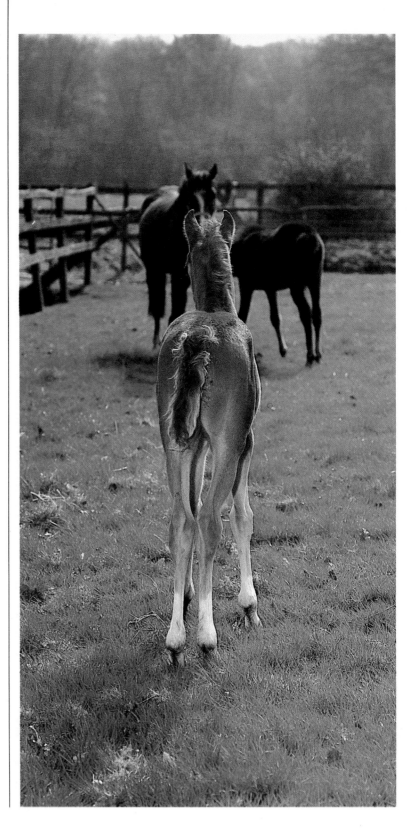

Dresden watching Brandy and Whisky. The two foals would like to get together and are very curious about one another. But their mothers break up any overtures of friendship between the two.

Diary · Fifteen days

The rest of the Pitchwood mares and fillies lived in the park meadow on the far side of Dresden's paddock. There was one more mare due to foal, several two-year-old and yearling fillies, and a shifting population of visiting mares. Dresden was therefore surrounded by ponies of all ages, part of a herd, yet insulated from the aggressive tendencies of any of them.

Dresden has been watching the ponies in the meadow. He whinnies in greeting as one of the mares comes towards the fence.

Ponies are extremely social animals. They prefer to live in groups and hate solitude, and within the group each individual is involved in a complex network of relationships with all the others. When a young foal meets other ponies for the first time it is an exciting moment, and an important one. Without this social contact early in its life a foal will have difficulty acquiring the social skills needed to become a full member of the herd.

The first reaction to the sight of other ponies is intense interest and curiosity, but tempered with caution. Dresden stood quite still and watched. He could see the other ponies quite clearly, although his vision is different from that of a human. A pony's eyes are on the sides of its head. It can see almost all round, but there are two blind spots, directly in front for a distance of about 6 feet (2m), and directly behind, and it may have to move its head to focus properly on nearby objects.

If other ponies excited Dresden's curiosity, he also excited theirs and had to be examined. So they approached, and being much larger and more experienced than he, they were perfectly confident of themselves. This was a little worrying for Dresden, and he whinnied, uttering a cry that is somewhere between a welcoming nicker and a neigh of mild alarm, high-pitched because of his small size, but he stood his ground because the approaching ponies did not look threatening and mother was not far away.

Ponies are highly vocal, but sound is not their only, or even their main, means of communication. When individuals meet,

Diary · Fifteen days

All the ponies in the park meadow were as interested in Dresden as he was curious about them. Some of the mares, such as April Morning of Pitchwood, were old friends of Porcelain, and came up to the fence to sniff noses with her, as well as to inspect her foal. However, had the fence not been between them, Porcelain would not have allowed even friends to come closer to her foal. As it was, she suddenly decided to lead Dresden right away from the fence (see p. 24).

Porcelain had been away from Pitchwood all last autumn and winter, and had only been brought back when due to foal. Ponies have very good memories for old friends, and old enemies too. By sniffing noses over the fence friendships were quickly re-established, but old enmities could only be sorted out when no physical barrier existed.

the rituals of greeting and inspection are conducted in silence.

Dresden, being a very junior member of the band, took no risks. He mouthed his submission first and waited to be invited before taking liberties, but submission is not the same thing as fear, and he was not frightened. His ears were pricked forward, showing keen attention and interest. With Porcelain beside him he was quite safe. Were he to approach an adult he might well have been rebuffed for his impertinence. On one occasion he was even kicked by another foal, though he was not really hurt.

Were he part of a group of wild ponies this stage would not last long. He would learn quickly what was permitted. He could play with his mother, of course, and with other foals of his own age. Wild stallions, too, are generally tolerant and playful with foals. They enjoy a bit of a chase and a mock tussle.

It takes time for a young foal to learn all the facial expressions and body postures by which ponies indicate their intentions and emotional state and until it understands these it relies mainly on its nose to investigate its surroundings. When he met another animal Dresden had to sniff it thoroughly, and he examined humans in the same way. Once he had completed his examination he would remember the smells he found. Ponies are renowned for their memories. If Dresden meets the same individual again a sniff will remind him, and if the encounter was especially pleasant or unpleasant he will remember and probably react to that, too.

Matters are rather more complicated when two adults meet. They are intensely curious about one another, but cautious. Questions must be answered and reactions predicted. Ponies are peaceable animals, but you can never be entirely certain. There are aggressive individuals, and nervous ones, and a sudden fast kick from a foreleg can do considerable damage.

The investigation begins, and may end, with a careful look and listen. The pony may move its head to get a better view and its ears will point forward to catch any sound. An object that moves may be another pony, and then again it may not be. That is the first thing to decide. If it looks like a pony, does it make any sound and, if so, are they pony sounds? If the object is not a pony, is it known to be friendly? A human friend can be recognized, and so can another familiar animal that the pony knows is harmless, and perhaps likes. It may approach a friend, but if it fails to recognize the animal it will take the safest course, and move out of the way, thus ending the investigation.

If the other animal is a pony, then how is it holding its body, and especially its neck and head? What is the position of its ears, and what expression is it giving with its mouth? These will indicate whether or not it is friendly. If it looks unfriendly, the best thing is to move out of its way, but if it seems friendly it can be investigated more closely.

This approach is made slowly, and stops when the ponies are

still several metres apart, because the 'flight area' of one pony has touched that of the other. The flight area extends beyond the personal space. Crossing into it alerts the pony, makes it suspicious, and may cause it to escape. Neither may advance beyond this point except by mutual consent. The two may recognize one another by sight or voice, but if not they will sniff each other's noses, usually standing at a slight angle rather then directly head on, so that each of them will be able to see clearly the ear, mouth and other facial signals that follow this initial contact. If the two recognize one another as old friends they will relax, no further introductions being necessary. If not, the mutual investigation must continue.

Porcelain and April sniff noses; their encounters over the fence are amicable. Dresden is hesitant about approaching another adult; he waits, mouthing, for the adult to approach him. But the fence is in the way.

Diary · Seventeen days

A misty start promised a really warm day at last, but the mist was slow to clear over the south side of Pitch Hill. All the mares with foals had been put out into the big field together. They would stay there for the summer, unless the weather turned cold and wet again, when they might have to come in at night.

At first the mares were all busy with the fresh grass, and the foals explored or whizzed around their mothers. However, all was not as peaceful as it seemed. The old mare, Peepshine, soon started to reassert her dominance over Porcelain, and especially sought her out to chivvy her. Porcelain knew Peepshine meant trouble and ushered Dresden away to the other side of the field. But it was not long before Brandy and Mena noticed that Porcelain had found some better grazing, so joined her, and of course Peepshine soon followed, which drove Porcelain away again. Peepshine was the biggest mare with foal, so could boss anyone. Brandy and Mena didn't let themselves be pushed around, but Porcelain, having been away from Pitchwood for six months, was naturally less self-confident and allowed herself to be bullied by Peep. The foals, too, came in for some bullying from her; she cornered Whisky once, knocked him down and pummelled him with her forefeet. He quickly scrambled to his feet and bellowed for his mother, but he wasn't really hurt. Whisky was a very naughty little colt, so he could well have deserved to be put in his place by Peepshine.

When two stallions meet as strangers they perform a ritual all their own. They snort, flex their muscles, and generally make themselves look big, fierce, and extremely important, slowly circling each other as they do so. Then one of them will find a pile of dung, sniff it ostentatiously, then deposit more dung on top of it. This plants his personal smell firmly on the pile he now calls his own. It demonstrates his authority, but the other stallion follows suit, planting his smell over the top. Usually the strange contest ends when one stallion admits he is beaten and walks away, leaving the last contribution, and therefore the pile, to his rival.

If the two are not both stallions, and strangers, there may be a little flirting between ponies of opposite sexes, while between two mares or two young animals the sniffing will continue, provided both of them want it. If one loses interest the encounter ends, and they separate. If not, sniffing extends from noses to faces, to shoulders, to sides, to rumps, and eventually to the entire body.

By this time the two will have established an acquaintance. If they were humans they might talk politely about the weather, their families, holidays, and other uncontroversial matters. The pony equivalent is mutual grooming, which really amounts to the same thing. If they are both youngsters they will not be much interested in small talk and will prefer to play, so they will start a game.

Encounters are not always friendly, even among ponies, but they rarely lead to fights. On the open grasslands there is plenty of room and confrontations are easily avoided simply by moving out of range. Individuals that dislike one another, for ponies do have friends and enemies, can and do keep out of each other's way as much as possible.

Ponies are intensely curious about strangers. Members of a herd know one another well, of course, and most wild herds are family groups. Nevertheless, opportunities to meet strangers do occur. One herd may encounter another by chance and while the stallions try to separate them, mainly to prevent the theft of mares, the mares themselves may be busy making new acquaintances. Now and then they may also came across an exciting band of colts wandering far from their own herd in search of mares to form herds of their own.

Mothers rarely allow other ponies too close to their foals. The mother may threaten what she regards as the intruder, who usually withdraws rather than risk a fight. The alternative is for the mother to move away herself, taking her foal with her. When Porcelain tried this technique it was not an unqualified success. The other pony, a grown-up mare with a foal of her own and who should have known better, failed to understand the obvious message, or chose to ignore it. She persisted in her approach and it turned into something of a chase.

Porcelain making her escape around the edge of the big field to get away from the old bully, Peepshine. Dresden has to canter to keep up with his mother's trot.

Peepshine hounding Porcelain, getting between her and Dresden, who squeals and mouths at her. Porcelain lashes out at Peepshine, who flings up her head to avoid the kick, allowing Porcelain to escape.

Living in a group

When he was not sleeping or eating Dresden spent most of his time playing or searching for possible playmates. He played with Porcelain, who was very patient, so he had no hesitation in trying to wake her when she was sleeping but he wanted her to join in one of his games. When he bumped into her neck while she was grazing, pretended he was not looking where he was going, then compounded the offence by stopping to scratch his nose, Porcelain showed a touch of exasperation. She had to interrupt her feeding and step round him and her momentary bad mood showed in her face. Her ears pointed a little to the side. This suggested she was feeling tired, perhaps because Dresden had already disturbed her rest. The ears also pointed slightly to the rear. This showed irritation. If they were laid right back she would be threatening him. Dresden had to learn these signals if he was to become a full member of the group, and he

Porcelain puts her ears back in annoyance as Dresden pauses beneath her chin. But she is not threatening him; if she had been really angry her ears would have been flat back.

learned them from Porcelain and from the other foals.

The foals loved racing, and chases that involved rapid, tight turns at full speed, and the colts enjoyed mock battles. Their mock fights were rehearsals for the challenges with which they may meet rival stallions when they are adults. Such play-fights can get out of hand and turn into serious contests when high spirits give way to flashes of real anger. If there are enough foals in the herd they soon tend to organize themselves into separate colt (male) and filly (female) groups, each group playing its own games, although mixed-sex herds sometimes develop.

The separation of the sexes usually starts early, and when they grow up this is the way most of the ponies will live. The usual herd, which is basically a family group, consists of one adult stallion, usually about four mares, although a stallion may have up to as many as twenty, and youngsters of both sexes up to

Diary · Four weeks

Often when Porcelain was grazing, Dresden seemed deliberately to walk into her neck, so she had to lift her head over his back to let him pass under his chin, then put her head down again to go on grazing. This morning, the same thing occurred, but Dresden, instead of going on walking, stopped to rub his muzzle against the inside of his knee. Porcelain was definitely annoyed. She had to step round him before she could continue her interrupted grazing.

Porcelain lies down beside Dresden while he is still standing (usually he is already asleep before she goes down). He gets very coltish and playful, pawing her back and gnawing her mane.

47

Diary · Four weeks

The mares with foals had been joined in the big field by some other mares. This morning the yearlings and two-year-olds were put in with the herd. Some of the older ponies resented the youngsters, so there was tremendous excitement and milling around for a while, till they had all sorted themselves out. They then settled down to grazing, in their own groups.

Far right *Three yearling fillies, Fi, Fern and Barbie,* right *canter around the big field, keeping in a close bunch.* Below *the whole herd milling about; Porcelain trots excitedly with tail high. In the confusion Dresden becomes separated from his mother* below right. *He calls her, anxiously showing the whites of his eyes.*

about two years old. Stallions that have no mares form herds of their own, and herds can form that have no stallion.

The stallion is not a leader, in the sense of being dominant over the mares; ponies are much more democratic than that. The stallion herds the mares, to keep them together, so when they are on the move he is more likely to be at the rear than in the lead. They are safer while they stay close together, and he is anxious not to lose any members. If there is danger, all the ponies will run, but the stallion will rush out to challenge any other stallion that comes too close and might try to abduct one of his mares. His herding and defence of the herd can make him look like a leader, but he is not aggressive to his own family.

Some ponies are more aggressive than others, so a kind of hierarchy can develop within the group, with bullies and submissive individuals, but the bullies are not leaders, they are just bullies. Ponies like to follow one another when they are on the move and it is that which keeps the group together.

Colts are more playful than fillies, and their games can also include herding, provided there is something to be herded. They will herd sheep, chickens, and any other suitable animals, but should not be allowed to do so. They are clumsy and careless with animals smaller than themselves and may trample members of their 'play herds'.

Communication

When the excitement of the morning had died down the fillies wandered about the field. Several of them had met their own mothers for the first time since last summer. April had recognized her yearling daughter Barbie, and seemed pleased. But Brandy, because of Whisky, had not been pleased to see her two-year-old Tootsie. The fillies, in their turn, were mildly aggressive towards any foals they met, no doubt establishing their own dominance.

Dresden mouthing submission as he retreats from the slightly threatening advances of Lady Bird, a two-year-old filly. She will not follow him once he is within Porcelain's private space.

Ponies communicate with one another constantly, vocally, and by scent, but mainly by facial expression and body posture. Some of their signals are direct messages; others are more or less involuntary and indicate their mood.

The neigh of a stallion is different from that of a mare. A neigh is usually used to find or summon another pony to come closer and be identified, and it may indicate mild alarm. Nickers are used by mothers to summon their foals, by ponies to call a friend closer, and in courtship, but only at very close quarters, like a friendly greeting. A mare will whinny to call her foal when it has wandered too far from her or she has lost sight of it, and a whinny carries a long way. A very excited stallion may snort his challenge at a rival, and the snort will alert the whole herd so it is ready to move at short notice, but he may also snort at any strange object, or just in high spirits. A pony that is very angry, or terrified, will scream or roar. If colts that are play-fighting begin to scream, the fight has become real.

The way a pony feels affects the way it holds its body, and this is the key to its very expressive body language. The more excited it is the more it will tense its muscles, and its neck and back will look curved. It will look excited, and this kind of posture will excite other ponies that see it. The curved outline can be

emphasized still more by the way the pony holds its tail, from a roughly horizontal position of alertness to high over the back. Raising the tail high can be a signal to gallop. If the pony is relaxed, its body will be straighter and, except when the pony moves it to dung or urinate, the tail will hang limp.

The ears are very mobile and because they are also highly visible they are invaluable. In their relaxed position, in which a pony has all-round hearing, the ears are upright and facing to the sides or slightly to the rear. They can be turned to face the direction to which their owner is paying most attention, and a pony listening to its rear may expect to be disturbed from that quarter. It is a sign of nervousness, but also of submission. With ears facing forward a pony is interested in whatever is in front, and this is the position for greeting. Ears can also be held erect or flattened. Erect ears mean the pony is confident. Half-lowered ears are a sign of nervousness or submission, and when the ears are laid back flat the animal is either very frightened or very angry.

A pony has large lips that can be curled back far enough to seal the nostrils, as in the flehmen response to a particularly interesting smell, often of sexual significance, and the mouth and nose also convey messages. In general, the more relaxed the

How do you tell yawning from mouthing? Dresden appears to be mouthing at Porcelain, but he is only yawning. His tongue is out a bit and he is about to close his eyes, something he would never do while mouthing.

pony the more relaxed will be its mouth, for tension often shows first in the face. In the mouthing response by which a foal shows submission to an adult, the mouth is opened part-way, almost like the start of a yawn. If an adult opens its mouth to another pony just a little it may indicate an invitation to mutual grooming. After that, the wider the mouth the more aggressive the message, and a pony that displays its teeth may be about to bite. Flaring nostrils indicate exertion or excitement, but a pony can also wrinkle its nose, much like a human does, to express disgust or irritation.

Far left Porcelain smells Dresden who turns his head to greet her. Mare and foal still need to check each other's scent quite frequently; they cannot be sure of recognizing one another by sight alone.

Below Porcelain lies dozing while Dresden is stretched out in deep sleep. Only a mare and her foal, or two very close friends, will sleep so near to one another.

Diary · Four weeks

Five foals were due to be born at Pitchwood Stud this year. The last to arrive was Pitchwood Princely Gift (stable name Prince). His mother was the bay Tetworth Soubrette. Although the weather was warm and fine, the pair remained in the foaling box for the first few days, to allow Prince time to become firmly imprinted on his own mother. Today Soubrette and Prince had been turned out into the big field, but they kept well away from everyone else, which meant Soubrette had to be content with the bits of the field less favoured by the other mares. The four older foals and the yearlings were all very interested in the newcomer, but Soubrette warned them off each time they approached, and led Prince away to the far end of the field.

Far right *Buttercups are distasteful to ponies, so the flowery parts of the field are less popular grazing areas. However, Soubrette finds peace there for herself and her new foal Prince, away from the other inquisitive and bothersome ponies.*

Communications are elaborate, and most unpleasant confrontations can be avoided, but this is not to say that a pony herd is necessarily free from bullies or that some foals are not more adventurous than others in their explorations. Among wild ponies, though, bullying is probably uncommon. Bullying is the product of crowding and competition for scarce resources, such as food, and in open country it is rare. There is always room to move and even if food is scarce it is usually distributed over a wide area, so individuals tend to disperse to find it.

An adventurous foal may always be the first to rush off in search of new games or new places to explore, and the others will often follow. This makes one foal into a leader and the others into followers, but as with the adults the leadership is not based on violence or threats of it.

Newcomers are a source of great excitement, but in the confined space of a field the excitement can lead to hopeless confusion. When ponies meet they must examine one another, find out whether they know one another, are or could be friends and, if they are youngsters, whether they might play together.

The trouble is that the entire herd may want to investigate the new arrivals all at the same time. For their part, the newcomers will be nervous. They are heavily outnumbered, may not be welcome by at least some members of the herd, and it is impossible for them to tell potential friends from enemies when the others all come at them together in a rush. So they try to slow things down by moving out of the way, but there is nowhere for them to go so they start running. This makes the herd chase them, and soon all the ponies are rushing frantically all over the place, trying to catch up with one another, to greet one another, to avoid one another, and for a short while social order collapses into anarchy. This is, fairly literally, a 'mêlée', the word used in medieval times to describe a tournament in which all the riders contested together, each against all, amid just such confusion.

In the course of all the rushing around some foals are separated from their mothers. This causes genuine distress, and the foals show the whites of their eyes. Ponies show the whites of their eyes when they are looking to the rear. It is not necessarily a sign of alarm, although it gives them a startled appearance, but any fright or worry automatically alerts the animal to the risk of attack from behind, the direction from which a predator is most likely to approach, and where it is most difficult to see. Ponies have not lived with humans long enough to forget their fear of wolves and large cats.

The lost foal cries its distress and its mother recognizes its particular voice, and responds. The foal probably cannot tell the call of its own mother from that of other mares, but it moves in the general direction of the sound, the cry and response being repeated like homing signals until the two are finally reunited.

Friendship and sex

At four weeks old Dresden is an active, playful colt, about to take the next big step in his life. He is ready to start making special friends from among his playmates. Friendships he makes now are likely to be close and to endure for many years.

We will see him begin to put into practice all the calls, greetings, facial expressions and body postures he has been learning. Soon he will be communicating his feelings fluently, and understanding the messages he receives from others. His increased fluency will make him more self-confident in company.

While Dresden is making friends, other relationships are developing within the group. Although he is much too young to have a mate himself it is now May, and the time of year when new foals are conceived, to be born the following spring. Dresden will watch as the adult ponies, including Porcelain and his own father, Fidelity, court one another and then mate, and he will react to the specifically sexual scents the grown-ups emit.

Fidelity is nuzzling up to Porcelain. Stallion and mare blow into each other's nostrils and smell each other's scented breaths. Suddenly the mare squeals and tosses her head. Fidelity squeals too. Again they sniff each other's nostrils. Again they both squeal. This little game may be repeated several times; it is part of the courtship ritual.

Mating

Porcelain was due in season again, as it was three weeks since her foaling heat. Mares are not covered during the foaling heat, which occurs a few days after the birth of a foal, but are put to the stallion during the second season, a month after foaling. Fidelity, the stallion, was led to the field to 'try' Porcelain. Her lack of reaction showed she was not yet ready, but several other mares crowded over to the fence and displayed to him. Two days later Porcelain was in season, and during the next three days was covered by Fidelity several times.

April, in season, flehms after smelling the urine of her in-season filly friend, Pavlova. The grimace is often known as 'stallion face'; it is relatively unusual for a mare to flehm.

Mares will mate between March and September and, although stallions are able to mate during the winter, during the mating season they secrete more of the male hormone testosterone. This makes the muscles of their neck and shoulders grow larger, and it alters their temperament. They posture a great deal, as though boasting of their prowess to any pony who cares to notice and especially to possible rivals. A stallion will rarely mount a mare, however, unless she invites him to do so. Despite his energy and physique, mating is under the control of the mare. When she is ready she will seek him out. In a wild herd, of course, there will be only one stallion for her so she cannot choose a mate from among a number of suitors.

During the season a mare will come into heat about every three weeks, for a period of about five days, but the cycle is very irregular. It can vary for an individual mare, and from one mare to another. She ovulates on the last day but one of her heat.

As she comes into heat the mare will secrete substances that alter the smell of her urine. This will excite the stallion, who will sniff and show flehmen when he encounters it, the flehmen sometimes leaving his nose running so he has to snort to clear it. Mares will also show flehmen at the scent of another in-heat mare, but this is less common. This communication by scent probably works on both sexes. The smell of the female excites the male, but she may also need his smell to modulate her own hormonal activity.

At first the mare will flirt, but without letting the stallion come too close. She will walk past his head, so he cannot help picking up her scent, and as she passes she will quickly flick her tail aside and let it fall again, giving him a brief glimpse of pink in a 'wink' of invitation. If he tries to accept the invitation she will squeal or kick or simply run a short distance out of reach.

Her flirting drives the stallion into his courtship ritual, which is impressive. He arches his neck, tucks in his chin close to his chest, lifts his tail jauntily, and goes into a prancing dance, lifting his feet high, as he circles what he hopes will be his prize. In fact he is being tortured by conflicting impulses. He wants to seize the mare and mate with her, but he dare not. To do so would mean invading her personal space and his whole experience of life has taught him never to do that without a clear invitation. If he were to invade, the mare might well kick him savagely, and he would deserve it. It is the confusion caused by the conflict that explains the dance.

He dances to his mare until at last he persuades her to stand still and allow him to come close to her. Only then may mating begin.

Individual courtships vary greatly, however, just as they do among humans, and some in-season mares are more enthusiastic about mating than others. Jealousies may also arise, with one mare trying to keep the stallion to herself.

Fidelity neighs forcefully to the mares in the field. His running nose shows he has also been flehming; a stallion often snorts moisture away after flehming.

Porcelain looks round as Fidelity neighs, but affects indifference. She is just coming in season, but not enough to respond by tail-raising and urinating like the other in-season mares. In another two days she will be showing.

Diary · Five weeks

It was a brilliant sunny day after a wet weekend, and Porcelain was in season. Accompanied by Dresden, she had been brought to Fidelity for the covering, in the bluebell-wood paddock alongside the big field.

Porcelain stands with her head in as Fidelity approaches. His neck is proudly arched as he nuzzles her. Dresden is apprehensive at such an obviously powerful and dominant adult coming close to him and his

mother. He keeps on the far side of her away from Fidelity and mouths with an audible suckling noise. But Fidelity is not taking any notice of the foal at the moment; he is totally preoccupied with Porcelain!

For the covering Porcelain needs to be held in just her head collar, but Fidelity has a bridle with straight-barred bit and keys, to give him something to play with, with his tongue. The chain is needed to control his stallion impetuosity.

Dresden is fascinated by Fidelity, as well as being nervous of him. He keeps very close to Porcelain but peeps at the stallion round her neck and under her belly. All the time he keeps up a constant mouthing, to placate the big and possibly dangerous stranger. Even when he is hiding round the other side of his mother, Dresden's message is transmitted to Fidelity, because mouthing is not only an eye-catching signal, it is an audible one as well.

Pony courtship consists not only of nuzzling and smelling, but also of nipping and kicking. When the covering takes place in hand, nibbling and biting are allowed, but kicking is discouraged as far as possible. Here, Fidelity is reaching down to nip Porcelain's leg. Had the pair been at liberty, Porcelain would probably have responded by kicking him, but, as it is, she has to put up with quite a hard nip without being able to retaliate.

Mare and stallion are no strangers, so courtship need not be lengthy. Porcelain invites Fidelity to mount her by standing stock still in typical 'sawhorse' posture with her tail raised. She urinates and 'winks' with eye-catching pink flashes of her vulva. Fidelity smells her urine and flehms *below, breathing the smelly air up into his nose with a sucking, hissing noise. As he mounts Porcelain, he nibbles at her* withers *bottom.*

*His mounting pushes her forward;
she backs as she braces herself,
kicking up ashes from an old fire.
Dresden runs round and round
them, unsure where safety now lies.*

The stallion will greet his mare, nose to nose in the proper manner, then start grooming her gently, attentively, along her face and neck, shoulders, and side, so working his way towards the rear, all the while nickering quietly but insistently, persuasively. As he comes within reach of her hind legs he steps back a little, but licks and nibbles at her flank and leg and sniffs her. She will have been urinating in short spurts and as he approaches her tail he will sniff at the urine and show flehmen again. At this point the stallion becomes fully aroused sexually.

It may all be too much for the mare, especially if she is inexperienced. In that case she may move away nervously and perform a short dance of her own, then stop and urinate again. Or she might squeal, stamp or kick. Faced with such rejection the stallion will begin his own dancing approach all over again.

If she is ready and prepared to receive the stallion, the mare will stand still, braced to take his weight on her back, and move her tail to one side. He will mount, often steadying both of them by holding her shoulder with his teeth, in most cases quite gently. Several attempts may be needed before the two mate successfully, but when they do it is completed in less than a minute. The ponies separate and, for a time, go their own ways. They usually mate again, however, later the same day, and sometimes less than an hour later, when the mare may be more insistent in her soliciting than she was the first time.

Courtship and mating are complicated by the webs of personal relationships within a herd of ponies. Some ponies are jealous of others, and some are nervous and this can make them irritable. Even when she is not in heat a jealous mare might drive other mares away from the stallion. The stallion himself may well have favourite mares, and other mares he always ignores. Many stallions prefer mares of a particular colour and will have nothing to do with others.

Other difficulties are caused by ignorance. Communication is extremely important. The stallion must understand the messages he receives from the mare, and must approach her reassuringly, entering her personal space with caution and delicacy, making the correct gestures of friendship and conciliation. The mare must recognize these and, when the time comes, allow him to mount. Ponies that have been raised as a group, in the company of older animals of both sexes since they were foals, learn how to behave. Those raised by themselves, or entirely among members of their own sex, may not, and formidable problems may emerge. Young stallions may be so alarmed by the response of a mare they have frightened as to be totally inhibited. Others may be so eager they become violent and risk injuring the mare and themselves. Among domesticated ponies ample time is allowed for the stallion and mare to become acquainted, then friendly and relaxed in each other's company, before they are allowed to start courting.

Diary · Five weeks

Porcelain will be 'tried' again when her next season is due, in another three weeks' time. If she fails to 'show' by displaying to the stallion, it will be safe to assume that she has 'taken' and is in foal. Gestation is approximately eleven months, so Porcelain's next foal should be born close to Dresden's first birthday. After the covering Porcelain and Dresden rejoined the herd in the big field and Fidelity returned to his own paddock. With the mares and fillies in season, the three colt foals in the herd were showing precocious stallion behaviour. Whisky, the eldest, was a particularly naughty colt, though all three showed interest in the mares. They were starting to moult out of their baby fur. Whisky's whole face was already showing his adult colour, but Dresden as yet only had dark rings round his eyes and a dark muzzle of the sleeker chestnut adult coat.

After the covering Fidelity turns his attention to his son, reaching over Porcelain's back to sniff and nibble Dresden's rump – to the foal's consternation. Stallions are naturally interested in foals and kindly disposed towards them.

Adolescence

A spell of fine weather was forecast, at last. In the big field the colt foals were being very coltish again. They all made stallion faces several times during the morning, after smelling urine, either from their own dams or from one of the fillies. All the foals were still eating fresh dung from their own mothers – even Whisky, who surely must have had his gut flora well established by now.

Whisky stretches his neck out and flehms after smelling mare's urine. The foals do not point to the skies when flehming, as the mature stallion often does.

As a member of a group if not of a wild herd, Dresden had ample opportunity to learn the correct way to behave, and the lesson will stand him in good stead when the time comes for him to court a mare. He will await an invitation from a mare he knows well, then approach her courteously and with great delicacy. The better the couple know each other the more likely it is they will understand the extremely subtle personal messages that will pass between them, for every pony is a unique individual.

Dresden's lessons were based largely on observation, but they were mixed inextricably with his own feelings, and these made him behave in ways that were quite new to him.

He found himself drawn irresistibly to the smell of urine, and in particular to the urine left by mares. When he sniffed it he raised his head, stretched his neck forward, pulled back his upper lip until it covered his nostrils and so partly sealed his nose, and stood there, quite still, for a few moments, holding his breath. This was flehmen.

Flehmen is seen most often among ponies when a male smells the urine of a mare, and especially of a mare who is in heat, and very young colts flehm often, perhaps in response to their mothers' urine, but its significance is not only sexual. A pony

will flehm at any strange smell and, although no one can be certain, it appears to be nothing more than a way of giving a new or interesting smell a thorough examination. A pony relies on its sense of smell to identify things that are good to eat, so it may be wise to investigate possible food carefully. Dresden did not flehm as much as some foals. A filly foal has been known to flehm repeatedly when only one day old.

There were others ways, though, in which Dresden began to behave in a more adult fashion. When he smelled a mare's urine he flehmed, and then raised his head and tail, in a parody of a stallion's display of self-importance, and urinated. This was not so much a sexual signal, connected with mating, as one meant to enhance his own male social status.

Urine and dung convey messages, and so they can be used deliberately. When the bedding in a stall is changed a stallion often urinates on it at the first opportunity, perhaps to impose his own personal smell on it and make it his own. When he finds the dung of another stallion he will leave dung of his own on top of it, and when he finds dung or sometimes urine left by a mare he will urinate over it. To another member of the herd, the message means, 'I have been this way'.

Dresden above *wrinkles his nose as he starts to flehm. Curling the upper lip narrows the nostrils without closing them, so air is breathed in through narrow slits with an audible hiss. While flehming* below, *and with his tail raised horizontally, he stales on the mare's urine patch.*

Diary · Two months

Pitchwood Pavlova, the two-year-old Palomino filly, was in season again. She was too young to be put in foal yet, but came in season every month throughout the summer. She made a nuisance of herself to the other ponies, by crowding up close and inviting play and mutual grooming.

Porcelain is very intolerant of close approaches from anyone other than her own foal. She lunges at the importunate Pavlova with teeth bared and ears flat back.

A stallion prefers to dung in a particular place and the pile probably marks the area occupied by him and his herd. Ponies do not have territories as such, but this marking may help reduce conflict among rival stallions and competition for food between neighbouring herds.

Meanwhile there was much for Dresden to observe. As the adult mares came into season they began to regard one another jealously. One mare would drive away another with angry threats. A threat may be aggressive, in which case it is made from the front, or defensive, made from the rear with warning of a kick from the hind legs. These were aggressive threats, meant seriously, lunges made with the ears laid back in rage, the mouth open and the teeth bared.

The mares will flirt with any male, even with a young colt if his interest can be aroused, and usually it can. Even very young colts can be interested in sex. So far as the colt is concerned, and young observers such as Dresden, the encounter forms an important part of their education. As he approaches, the mare may turn from him, squeal, threaten to kick him, and move away, but skittishly, with her ears turned to the rear so she can hear whether he follows. The colt must learn how to approach without giving offence or being attacked, and how to react to this simultaneous rejection and invitation.

Left *Pavlova threatens to kick Whisky when he approaches. Her ears are back and she is squealing. He also squeals, nimbly sidestepping out of her way. She is only playing hard to get.*

Below *Pavlova, in love again, has approached Whisky too near his mother. Brandy quickly moves in to part the flirting pair.*

Social life

Diary · Two months

The foals had long ago given up running fast individual circles round their dams – all except Prince, the youngest, who was still at that stage. They had started to play together, especially in the evenings. But this evening the whole gang of youngsters was just loafing in the shade. The weather had been hot, with thunder clouds looming.

Percy rests his chin playfully on Dresden's rump. The two foals are well matched, but Dresden is cautious of the dominant Percy. He makes a funny mouth, playful, but ready to indicate submission if need be.

For most of the time, life among the ponies was very peaceful. Ponies are not aggressive animals and although there are disagreements now and then, these can usually be resolved without much conflict. Actual fights are very uncommon in the wild, except on the rare occasions when one stallion tries to capture mares from the herd of another and refuses to desist when challenged. Quarrels occur rather more often among domesticated ponies if they are encouraged to compete. The encouragement may be unintentional. If food is provided in just one place there are obvious advantages in reaching it first; a narrow gate may force some individuals to give way to others, perhaps unwillingly, and rewards of titbits or affection may amount to favouritism and lead to jealousy.

The foals were still young enough to run to their mothers when called, and to mouth submissively whenever they met a strange adult, or one who looked at them crossly, but they spent much of their time together, standing around in small groups, or playing. The days were growing warmer, however, and when the sun shone brightly they sought the shade. The weather did not really trouble them unless it was very severe, and ponies prefer to be out in the open. When the wind drives the cold rain in almost horizontal sheets they find shelter on the lee side of a wall or hedge and even if they are free to enter their stables they rarely do so. They are animals of the plains, the open spaces, and suffer badly from claustrophobia. Although some domesticated ponies are comfortable inside a stable and enter willingly, wild ponies prefer to be outdoors. The hiding place that would give many animals a sense of security makes them feel trapped.

Far left *The foals and yearlings are mooching around together, away from their mothers and the older ponies. Dresden grazes while Percy reaches up to browse.*

71

The fact is, ponies spend most of their time just loafing, an activity, or absence of one, for which they all have a positive genius. They have special places for it. Often a particular loafing spot is not large enough to accommodate a whole herd of ponies, so the group may have to separate into smaller groups. Ponies often graze in small groups, too, foals play in small groups, and the composition of each group remains fairly constant. It is a group of friends, individuals who may not be especially close, but who know from experience they can get along together well enough without arguing. The ponies decide the arrangement for themselves and it minimizes the risk of quarrels.

As they idled away the long summer days the ponies devoted part of their time to grooming one another. It is a ritual with several purposes, and extremely important.

It is easy to think of the organs of the body as being contained on the inside, and hidden, but the skin that contains them is also an organ, the barrier that protects the body from attack and insulates it against heat, cold, and water, and it contains nerve endings, sensors to inform the animal of its surroundings. Skin and, in mammals, the fur covering it needs regular care. Obviously, parasites must be removed from it, so far as that is possible. It must be kept clean. Dirt may harbour parasites and, more important, it may block sensors. Fur insulates the body by trapping air in its layers, but it can do this only while the hairs lie smoothly, all in the same direction. A coat is made waterproof by oils and waxes secreted by glands just below the surface, and these protective substances must be spread evenly.

Cleaning and generally attending to the care of the skin and fur is called 'grooming', and all animals must do it, but there are several ways to groom, depending on the circumstances. If an animal feels a sudden irritation it will attend to it directly and as quickly and vigorously as necessary, as Dresden does when he scratches. If the irritation is mild, perhaps little more than a sensation that the skin could be more comfortable than it is, the response is different. It is as though the sensation serves only to suggest to the animal that a general, complete grooming would be a good idea. It pays no immediate attention to the area in need of attention, grooming the whole of its body in a leisurely fashion, starting always with the face and head, and dealing with the minor irritation only when it comes to it.

Grooming removes any discomfort, and because it produces a pleasant, comforting feeling animals often groom themselves when they are confused, frustrated, or need to be comforted for whatever other reason. Cats are the animals most often seen grooming themselves to cover confusion, or embarrassment when a manouevre meant to be elegant goes badly wrong, but all mammals do this, ponies included, and in our way so do we.

Most animals have some part of their body they cannot reach, however, so sometimes they need help. A pony can scratch with

Diary · Two months

It was interesting to see close friendship developing among the foals, and to note which older ponies were already friends. Foals that were friends had quite long sessions of mutual grooming, and ran around playfully together. Millie, the only filly foal, didn't seem to have a special friend of her own age, though she was exceptionally friendly with humans. Dresden, also, did not seem to have a particular friend, but ran with any of the other colts. Whisky most often played with Percy, as did Prince. In fact, Percy, tall and handsome, seemed to be the most popular choice of playmate with all the other colts.

Prince pals up with Percy. They stand together at the edge of the field in the last of the evening sunshine.

its hoofs, can roll, and soon learns to rub its back against a rough surface, and its mouth will reach most of its body, but rubbing and rolling do not provide the detailed, precise attention the coat needs. So they groom one another. Because grooming is comforting, grooming another individual comforts it and so mutual grooming, or 'allogrooming' is important socially. It is doubly comforting because mothers groom their infants, so being groomed by another individual has pleasant mental associations as well as satisfying a purely physical need.

A pony that wishes to be groomed approaches another pony with its mouth open a little, showing the lower teeth, or makes special movements with its mouth and jaws.

The two ponies then work in unison to groom one another, starting with the face, moving to the head, and then working along the flanks, nibbling, licking, and scratching with their teeth. When it is time to change sides their heads are dealt with for a second time. Ponies enjoy being groomed by human friends, and will often return the compliment if invited to do so, though not everyone enjoys the experience.

Mutual grooming brings comfort and so an offer to groom can be used to reconcile a quarrel or by a stallion to conciliate a nervous mare he wishes to court. Strangers will often groom one another once they have sniffed their introductions. The ritual is also used, and frequently, to cement friendships, and friendship is very important indeed.

When Whisky is not flirting with Pavlova or one of the other fillies in season, he most often chooses Percy to play with. He nibbles Percy's chest at the start of a mutual grooming session.

Special friends

Foals start making friends as soon as they are old enough to leave their mothers' sides long enough to meet one another. The friendships may not last, for foals can fall out as easily as children, but sometimes they do, and adult ponies also form friendships.

A stallion who is the only adult male in a wild herd also prefers to groom and be in the company of his special friends among the mares, and he is a friend to all the foals. They will be turned away by mares other than their mothers, but rarely by the stallion.

Like all social animals, ponies tend to follow one another. Foals follow their mothers, and may continue to do so even after they are weaned, which provides the basis for family groupings, but individuals also follow their friends. If a mother has a friend to follow, her foal and perhaps her yearling will accompany her, and the friend may also have offspring, so several family groups can merge. The domestication of ponies exploits their readiness to follow their friends, including human friends.

Within the groups there are leaders and followers, not so much because one individual bosses another as because one is more inquisitive, always wants to explore new places or examine strange objects, and so is the first to move. The herd might break up into these small groupings altogether, and the groups disperse, were it not for the stallion. He is the herder, and his herding brings back any group that wanders too far.

Diary · Two months

Peepshine had by now quite given up hounding Porcelain; the two mares even seemed to be friends at times, occasionally grazing almost head to head. Two of the yearling fillies, Barbie and Fern, always grazed very close to one another. Barbie (Pitchwood April Love) was the daughter of the big grey mare April, and Fern (Pitchwood Cover Girl) was Soubrette's last year's foal, therefore Prince's older sister. Barbie and Fern had run around together as foals, had been weaned together and had continued to do everything together ever since. They would lie down side by side, graze with heads nearly touching, and drink from the water trough together. The foals were not yet drinking water; they were still getting their liquids second-hand from their mothers.

Barbie and Fern drink together from the water trough. Only ponies that are as close friends as these two may put their heads together into the trough.

Summer days

Courtship and mating over for another year, the ponies settle down for the summer as the days lengthen and, hesitantly, for it is a poor summer, the temperature rises. There are hot days, and really hot weather has to be endured rather than enjoyed. Keeping cool presents problems for an animal as large as a pony.

Summer is also the time when insects are most active. Some insects merely annoy ponies, but others are actually harmful and can cause real pain and serious illness. As they laze in their field, Dresden and his friends help one another to deal with them as best they can.

Alliances have been made within the group and friends spend as much of their time together as they can, although Dresden has not yet found any special friend of his own. Then, when he is about five months old, gates are unbarred, the ponies are turned out to roam in another field, and a wide exciting new world is opened up for exploration.

Exploring Norman's field. Some of the Pitchwood ponies have been put in a big field where they have never been before. Bucking and kicking gleefully, they do a couple of quick circuits of their new domain, before settling, heads down, to demolishing the fresh grass. Here, on top of the downs, there are always cool breezes blowing, and the ponies are less troubled by the pestering flies of summer.

Heat and horseflies

Summer had come at last; we were in the middle of a heat wave. The ponies were suffering from the heat and the constant irritation of biting and tickling insects. The mares and fillies grazed or stood around in the shade; the foals grazed a bit, suckled, lay down to sleep, or just stood around, loafing and dozing. There was very little interaction, little play or mutual grooming during the day; I suppose it was just too hot.

Porcelain was definitely in foal. She had been 'tried' twice since the covering, and had not come back in season. She and Peepshine had settled into a state of watchful neutrality. Peepshine no longer went out of her way to hound Porcelain, and the two even grazed peaceably together at times. But usually Porcelain kept her distance from the older mare, and so avoided trouble.

Some of the Pitchwood ponies had been sold, but had not yet gone to their new homes. Whisky would be the first to go; being the earliest foal he would soon be ready for weaning. Percy would miss his friend and playmate, but soon team up with Prince. Mena and Millie had also both been sold, but they would not go for several weeks yet.

As the days grew warmer, the ponies had to spend some of their time just keeping cool. Muscles work best at around 38°C (101.5°F), and this is the normal body temperature of a healthy pony. When the muscles work they are supplied with energy by a chemical process that breaks down sugars carried in the blood. The process also generates heat, so all physical activity warms the body. Surplus heat must be removed, because a temperature only a few degrees higher than ordinary body temperature is lethal.

In hot weather the ponies move no more than is absolutely necessary. This is not laziness, but prudence. They must not generate body heat needlessly. Often they lie down, which places a large area of their skin directly in contact with the ground, allowing heat to be conducted from them. They choose shade if there is any, but even in the open the ground feels cool, and is cooling, and the pressure flattens the hairs of their coats, expelling the warm insulation of air trapped among them.

The blood vessels lying just beneath their skin dilate. This increases the flow of blood close to the body surface. The blood is warmed deep inside the body, but cooled while it passes beneath the skin. This, too, aids cooling. Ponies also sweat – profusely

In the middle of the day Dresden lies flat out in deep sleep while Porcelain stands over him, dozing and swishing her tail.

and most of the time. The evaporation of the sweat from the skin lowers its temperature. This loss of body fluid means they must drink a little more, but on the steppes and in the American west wild ponies need to drink only every two or three days, even in hot weather. They are well adapted for life in fairly dry climates, where pools and rivers may be hard to find, and they make efficient use of the moisture in the food they eat.

All mammals keep cool in much the same way, but large animals, such as ponies, find it more difficult than do smaller ones. Heat generated inside the body must be dissipated from the surface, so the larger the surface area in relation to the volume of the whole body, the more easily will heat be lost. The larger the animal, the smaller is its surface area in relation to its volume. This means that large animals retain body heat more efficiently than small ones, which is an advantage in cold weather, but a disadvantage on a hot summer day.

It is not surprising, therefore, that ponies are better than humans at keeping warm in winter, but that they are much less comfortable than we are in summer. The heat makes them miserable, but only during the middle of the day. They are more active around dawn and dusk.

Diary · Three months

This evening the ponies were all in the long meadow. At the far end, a fallen tree trunk was a focus of attention. Most of the branches had been broken off, but those that remained made good rubbing posts for the foals. They were all moulting. Whisky looked like an Apaloosa; his bleached foal coat was coming away in tufts, the dark adult coat showing through in spots and patches.

Four foals – Percy, Whisky, Millie and Prince – put their heads together over a rotting tree trunk, much gnawed and pawed by previous generations of foals. Porcelain and Dresden are keeping away from the gathering, because of Peepshine.

Most of the movements a pony makes while otherwise standing resting are meant to remove insects. Every now and then it will give a vigorous toss of its head to dislodge flies from its face. It may stamp, twitch its skin, or scratch by moving through dense vegetation.

It also swishes insects away with the long hairs that grow from its short, stumpy tail. Often friends stand side by side, nose to tail, so each can whisk away the flies from the face of the other and a pony may even tuck its head right beneath its friend's tail. Tail-docking deprives a pony of its whisk. Lacking fingers that can grasp objects, ponies rarely use tools, but a pony with a docked tail has been known to scratch itself with a stick held in its mouth.

Female horseflies suck blood which they obtain by stabbing their victim fiercely, but ponies seem to consider them no more than a minor irritant. Some people call them gadflies, but it is horse-bot flies, not gadflies, that set a pony racing around its field, 'gadding about' in terror. The fly lays her eggs painlessly on the pony's skin, the pony swallows them when it grooms itself, they hatch and complete their growth in its stomach, and then are excreted. They can cause illness and discomfort later, but no one knows why ponies fear the egg-laying females so much more than the blood-sucking flies.

Diary · Four months

What a dozy lot of foals today, not lying down but just standing, usually close to their mother's tails. They were very troubled by the flies, tossing their heads, stamping, licking, nibbling, rubbing their eyes on their own knees or on their mothers' hocks. In between, they moved along behind their mothers, close to the constantly fly-whisking tails. Mostly the flies were bothersome because they just tickled as they ran over the skin, drinking sweat. But occasionally a pony, mare or foal, became really agitated by a stinging fly, bucked and lashed out, then started running. The running seemed infectious, as if there'd been an invitation to play, or an alarm signal about the fly. All the ponies would cavort briefly, then run over to a clump of dense bushes where they would stand a while, heads in the deepest shade. Even there they were allowed no respite from the flies.

Far left *Dresden tossing his head to dislodge the flies. He looks very noble with his head up and showing the whites of his eyes – as if he ought to be signalling with a silent whinny to some distant pony. When flies get up his nostrils, he snorts as he tosses. Often he shakes his head to get the flies out of his ears. His mother's tail* left, *whisking flies from her own flanks, whisks them from his face as well. Above flies lapping moisture round Dresden's eye.*

81

Grazing

Dresden was still very leggy, though not as much as Percy who looked as if he was on stilts. To reach the grass, the foals now had a special grazing stance: instead of forelegs splayed sideways, giraffe-like, as when they were very young, they stepped one foreleg forward, one back, making an inverted 'V'. When they had grazed as much as they could reach within the 'V', they hitched their forefeet together again, walked forward a few paces, then repeated the manoeuvre.

With her relatively longer neck, Porcelain can reach the grass comfortably; she walks smoothly forward as she feeds, grazing in one continuous mowing motion. Dresden grazes with feet very wide fore and aft, in order to reach the grass.

Dresden was still suckling, an awkward operation that made him spread his forelegs wide apart in order to lower his head, while at the same time he had to raise his face upward to grasp the teat. He had been nibbling grass since he was just a few days old to augment the milk he received from Porcelain, and at two months old he grazed beside her just like an adult.

Watch a pony grazing and it may seem to be working its way fairly indiscriminately through the grass. In fact it is very selective about its food, and sorts through everything to find the items it prefers. Its head may be down, its nose in the grass, but it is using its very mobile upper lip to rummage in the herbage. It pushes aside the tougher, less tasty leaves and stems so its incisors can nip off the more succulent morsels.

It is very discriminating, but will eat a wide variety of plants. Wild ponies often live where the pasture is poor, so they cannot afford to overlook anything, and a domesticated pony grazes in the same way. It will eat grass, of course, but also fruit, buds, leaves from trees, acorns, the juicy young tips of gorse bushes, rushes, and even holly, thistles, briars, and tree bark if there is nothing else. A pony will not eat plants growing from a place

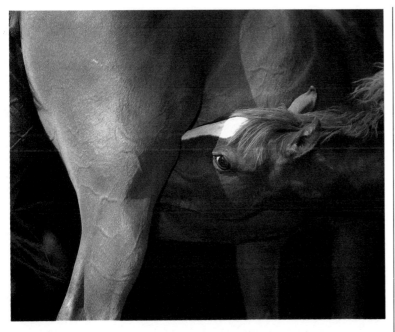

Dresden suckling. Although the foals eat quite a lot of grass now, they are still dependent on their mothers for much of their nourishment. They will not be weaned for another two months.

Below *Percy tongues around inside his lips after suckling, as if to savour the milk as long as possible.*

where ponies have urinated or dunged, no matter how lush the vegetation may be, but it will eat plants growing in cowpats. Ponies can tell the difference by the smell. As it grows older, however, a pony becomes more conservative in its tastes and may be very reluctant to try anything new.

Even when it is lush the food is not very nutritious, and a pony must eat a large quantity if it is to get the protein, carbohydrates, vitamins and minerals its body needs. Like most herbivores it must spend a great deal of its time feeding, precisely how long depending on the quality of the food. It will eat for a few hours, stop while it digests, then feed again when its appetite returns, which it will do more quickly if the last meal was a poor one.

Apart from eating when it is hungry, there is little regularity about a pony's habits. It does not have special times for eating and resting as do many grazing animals.

Its jaw muscles are large and strong and its teeth are adapted to crushing and grinding very coarse material. An adult pony has six incisors in each jaw, one or more very small premolars in the upper jaw, called 'wolf teeth', six premolars and six molars in each jaw, the premolars being very similar to the molars. A very few mares have rudimentary canines, but the great majority have none. Males have two canines in each jaw. The teeth grow continually and have very rough surfaces because the enamel, dentine and cement from which the teeth are made wear at different rates. Foals, like human children, have 'milk' teeth and wild ponies acquire the first of their permanent teeth when they are three years old.

Diary · Five months

Today was fine again, after an exceedingly wet weekend in the wake of a hurricane. The ponies were in the park meadow now. Suddenly the whole herd was pounding around, really running. The cause was Peepshine. This was the first time for a month that she had been in the same field as Porcelain, and she was determined to reassert her dominance. Percy didn't try to keep up with his mother, but Dresden ran with Porcelain, terrified.

When all the pounding around had died down, Porcelain kept well out of Peepshine's way. If she ever spotted her sauntering towards her with ears back, she quickly led Dresden to the other side of the field.

A pony has no trouble eating its food, but its digestion is less efficient than that of a ruminant animal, such as a cow. Its stomach is not divided into chambers, but like a ruminant it relies on bacteria to break down cellulose. These live in its caecum and large intestine, and food is stored temporarily in its fairly small stomach. The digestive system allows the pony to eat tough plant material, but not to digest it thoroughly, which is why horse dung contains much more fibrous matter than cow dung. The pony solves the problem by eating more than a cow and digesting its food quickly to make room for more.

While it grazes, with its head down, a pony must remain alert to danger, for it is in the open and clearly visible to predators. Its eyes do not focus sharply, but are adjusted in the centre of its field of vision to see objects in the middle distance clearly. At the top and bottom of the field its eyes are focused at infinity. This allows it to watch the horizon constantly, and it is acutely aware of the slightest movement.

Drinking is even more dangerous than eating, because in the wild many animals must converge to drink at what may be the only water in the area, and drinking places are favourite haunts for predators. A pony will pause in its drinking to raise its head for a look around. Learned in the wild, it is a habit few domesticated ponies have lost.

Dresden is fascinated by a puddle of rainwater. He will not step into it, but tastes it, sniffs it and blows on it from the safety of dry land.

Living as a member of a herd helps greatly. There are always one or two ponies on the look-out, with their heads raised.

Water is not only for drinking, however. A puddle is a curious object, and as such it must be examined closely. Dresden, blowing at the puddle he has found, will not step into it until he is quite certain there is no danger. He is not looking at the puddle, of course, for he cannot see anything as close as that directly to his front.

Meanwhile the social life of the ponies continued. They greeted and groomed one another, did battle with the flies, and now and then there was an argument that ended with one pony chasing away another.

Peepshine, with ears flat back and teeth flashing, reasserting her dominance over Porcelain. Dresden squeals with fear when trapped between her threatening teeth and his fleeing mother.

In show condition

Diary · Five months

The Pitchwood ponies had been doing well at shows, so we wanted to record Dresden and Fidelity in show condition. A plain dark background always sets off an animal to best advantage, so we brought Dresden and his parents to the indoor riding school at Glendale for the session. Fidelity and Dresden had been bathed and groomed; their manes were plaited and their hoofs oiled. The foal looked lovely, polished up and in a smart head collar, but he *hated* the silly rosette stuck behind his eye! He had lost nearly all his woolly foal's coat, and his bright chestnut summer coat was sleek and glossy. Fortunately he still had his whiskers, which contribute so much to a foal's

charm. Fidelity had had his whiskers shaved, but a foal is allowed to be whiskery for showing. Fidelity was magnificent, beautifully turned out, with shining coat and polished bridle, but I worried lest in the photographs he would be lost against the dark background. A liver chestnut coat absorbs light almost as much as a black. Anyhow, his rosettes would stand out well! Porcelain was the only pony not smartened up for the occasion. She is not a top quality brood mare, although she had been a champion as a filly and had won many times in classes for young stock. Of course she had to accompany Dresden otherwise he would have thrown tantrums and have been quite unmanageable without her.

Supreme Champion Keston Fidelity below, a fine example of his breed. A British Riding Pony, he looks like a small thoroughbred, with good withers to hold a saddle in place, strong quarters and good sound limbs. His head is very fine, with small ears and large kind eyes. His every movement expresses controlled power and his action is magnificent. In temperament, too, he is superb, for beauty of conformation must be matched by a kind nature and good manners; a riding pony must be suitable to be ridden by a child.

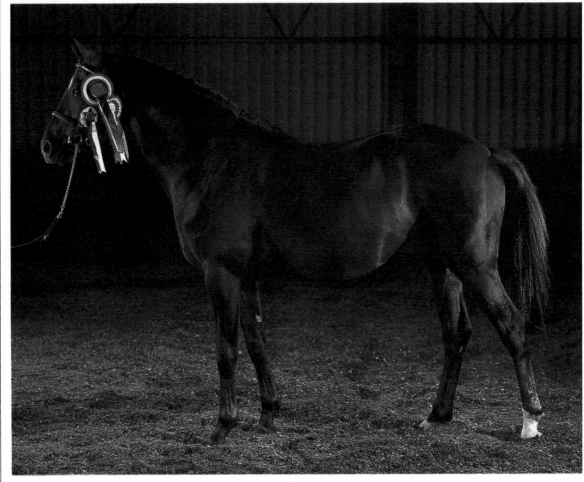

Pitchwood Dresden, though only a young foal, already shows definite potential as a show pony. He is not going to be quite as tall as his father; he will probably make 13.2 hh, whereas Fidelity stands 14.2hh and so has more substance than Dresden will have, and can carry a bigger child. It is hoped that Dresden will do very well in the yearling classes next summer and will follow in his father's footsteps eventually to become a supreme champion like Fidelity.

New horizons

We had been waiting for a fine spell to move some of the ponies to another field. The forecast was good for the next few days, so Porcelain and Dresden with Mena and Millie plus two fillies, Firle Eastern Surprise (Twiggy) and Pitchwood Fairy Footsteps (Tootsie), were brought over to Norman's field. This was just under the North Downs, between Weston Woods and St Martha's, with a line of mature conifers across its highest point. It was a beautiful morning, and our ponies were all bright and eager to explore. We had expected them to rush about in excitement all over the new field, where they'd never set foot before, but after a couple of high-speed and high-spirited rounds they just put their heads down into the long grass and kept them there for the next three days, with hardly a raised head in our direction.

By the end of the second day, Dresden and Millie had nearly had enough of grazing, and they would have played a bit and groomed each other, except that Tootsie seemed to be jealous of Millie and kept coming between them and spoiling whatever they were doing. And Mena also was inclined to break up their little games, especially if Porcelain was nearby. Porcelain must have been at the very bottom of the Pitchwood mares' pecking order, though Mena was nothing like so mean to her as Peepshine had been.

As the summer drew to its close and Dresden was almost five months old, some of the ponies were moved into a different field. There was a whole new world to explore, but the field was also covered in lush grass, and once through the gate the adventure turned into an extended meal. Only later, their hunger satisfied, did they begin serious exploration.

Usually, when ponies are turned into an unfamiliar field they walk all around its boundaries, following the fence or hedge closely. This seems to establish the enclosed area for them as one in which they can feed and move freely. It becomes their new range.

A 'range' is an area within which the ponies wander freely, but it is not necessarily exclusive. If other ponies enter, the area will not usually be defended, and among wild ponies the ranges of adjacent herds often overlap. A defended area, from which intruders are nearly always repelled, is a 'territory', and in the strict sense ponies are not territorial. It is not unknown for a stallion to drive away intruders, usually when several herds are crowded into a rather small area with many overlapping ranges, but probably he is merely anxious to prevent strangers from kidnapping any of his mares. It is not really territorial behaviour, although it may look like it.

Where ranges overlap, mares are inclined to wander from one herd to another, making it difficult or impossible for the stallion to guard them successfully. They will move when he herds them, so he can bring them together from time to time, but otherwise he has no real control over them, and there is nothing to stop one little group from drifting away while he attends to another or is otherwise engaged.

Sometimes herds will even mingle in order to loaf together in a large group, most often when the horseflies are at their worst. Individuals seem to be bitten less often while they are in large groups. The stallions tolerate this. After all, they benefit as much as the mares.

Among wild ponies, the size of a range depends on the resources the countryside offers. Where food and water are plentiful there may be up to thirty ponies to the square mile (twelve per square kilometre), and the average size for a range may be a little over 2 square miles (5 square kilometres). In harsher conditions the range may be around 10 square miles (26 square kilometres), with about five ponies in each square mile (three per square kilometre), to eke out a living from dry upland pastures or semi-desert.

The ponies will remain inside their range quite happily unless it is too cramped, they exhaust the food supply, or some other reason compels them to leave it. If their range comprises a field with good pasture, they will usually ignore broken fences they could easily cross, and even gates that have been left open. They are not especially interested in wandering for its own sake.

In the wild, though, ponies are quite likely to run out of food and hunger will make them move. They are nomads, and for the same reason that some people are nomads: there is no other way they can survive. A nomad recognizes no special place as a permanent home, is always open to a better offer, and ponies are typical. They are reluctant to move from a place where conditions are good to somewhere they know to be worse. When one has been taken to work in a place where the grass grows lush and juicy, it may see no sense in returning to its small, overgrazed paddock. If it likes its paddock and stable, on the other hand, it may see no sense in leaving them.

Pitchwood ponies grazing in Norman's field. Dresden and Millie, the only foals, have become close friends. Porcelain does not interfere, but Mena comes between the two foals, even when they are just grazing together.

Diary · Five months

Ponies can be about the most boring animals to try to photograph. Sometimes they seem to spend the entire time with their heads down. If there is any action, whether playful or aggressive, it tends to be brief, and over very quickly. To get action shots at all, one has to be prepared to follow the animals around the whole time while they are grazing, and be ready to grab the shot the instant anything happens, because it is most unlikely the ponies will ever repeat the performance.

Millie and Dresden had less need to graze non-stop; they obtained richer nourishment in a shorter time by suckling than the older animals did by non-stop grazing.

Above right Mena looks up briefly from her grazing, as Millie flings her heels in the air in a sudden burst of high spirits.

Below Dresden trotting along the crest of the hill to rejoin the herd. He has been exploring and finds himself being left behind as the others graze away from him.

Dresden was soon off exploring the new range, ears pricked and tail almost horizontal, showing he was very alert, stepping high in his excitement. He had to be cautious, for danger might lurk anywhere, so he felt a little conflict, fear of the unknown struggling against curiosity, and losing. In particular, he had to be extremely careful about the ground over which he moved. A false step, into deep mud, or water, or a hole, could trap him or lead to a broken limb, and in the wild either fate would mean certain death. The world is not a safe place for an animal with such long, thin legs, and ponies are wary about where they tread.

The remote ancestors of the modern pony were smaller than a wolf, lived in the forest, and had five toes, like most mammals. As the landscape changed and later descendants moved out on to the grasslands, little by little horse-like animals evolved which were better suited to the new way of life. A herbivore living in the open can be protected against predators by having a very thick skin, armament such as horns or tusks, or these can be sacrificed, along with the weight they represent, in favour of fleetness of foot and a strategy of evasion rather than self-defence. Pony breeds vary in size and the thickness of their skins, but all wild ponies are adapted for speed. No natural enemy can catch them but they have paid a high price.

A pony's legs are very long and its back is both long and supple. These give it a huge stride, which is the first part of the secret of its speed. As it moves, it throws its forelegs forward and pushes with its hind legs, so the powerful muscles that propel the animal are in its back and thighs. The upper parts of the legs above the knees, to which the big muscles are attached, are very short, but the lower parts are long and comparatively thin because tendons but no large muscles are attached to them; so they are light.

Humans walk on the soles of their feet with the toes pointing forwards. This is a 'plantigrade' gait. It is excellent for balance, but not very good for moving fast. Animals that run fast, such as cats and dogs, do so on the tips of their toes, with a 'digitigrade' gait. Ponies have taken the digitigrade gait to the extreme, and have reduced to the barest minimum the weight they must shift each time they lift their feet.

Instead of walking on the tips of all their toes, they walk on only one, the third. Vestiges of the second and fourth toes remain as small splint bones that do not reach the ground, but apart from these the pony has only one toe on each foot. Its toenails, consisting of pads made of several types of keratin, the general name for the materials from which skin, hair, feathers and horns are also made, have developed into hoofs, but the keratin is so arranged in the hoofs of a pony as to make it the toughest biological material known. In tests it has proved as strong as glass fibre reinforced with synthetic resins.

Keen senses that make it acutely aware of its surroundings, an ability to memorize a detailed map of the landscape all around so it always knows the shortest route to safety, an ability to survive on a poor diet and little water, combined with a long back and long, lightweight legs that allow it to outrun any predator, make the pony superbly adapted for life on the open grasslands. These are advantages. The disadvantage is that it is so highly specialized an animal it can do little else.

As the last ice age ended and the glaciers retreated, the forests spread and, unlike their remote ancestors, ponies cannot thrive in forests. Probably ponies were well on the way to extinction when humans first domesticated them. They had disappeared already from North America, where they had spent most of their evolutionary history. They died out there about 10,000 years ago, but starting in the sixteenth century, their domesticated descendants have been reintroduced by settlers from the Old World. Some then escaped from captivity, or were turned loose, to form the nucleus of the present American population of wild ponies, the 'mustangs'. Ponies descended from domesticated stock have also taken to living wild in Europe, including Britain, on Dartmoor, Exmoor, and in the New Forest. They revert very readily to their former way of life.

Ponies are nomads, but they are not migratory in the strict sense. They do not follow a circuit, moving by the same well-travelled routes from one place to another according to the seasons, as many animals do, and returning to the same areas regularly, year after year. When a herd of ponies abandons a range it simply moves on, with no intention of returning, searching always for better grazing. If it does return to the same place it is by accident. It was wandering such as this that took them from North America, across the land bridge that once linked Alaska to Siberia, and eventually to every part of the Old World except for isolated Australasia.

Where the range is large, however, ponies do cover long distances without leaving it, and their exploration of the range, followed by repeated visits to every part of it, maps it thoroughly for them. A pony has an excellent memory and associates places with events so it will return to somewhere it remembers as pleasant or rewarding, and try to avoid places where once it was hurt or frightened, but it does not rely exclusively on such emotional stimuli. It remembers countless details of its range and learns very quickly to find its way from one place to another without hesitation or mistakes. It knows the places where it will have a commanding view for miles around, the enclosed areas where it could be trapped, and, most important, the shortest route from anywhere to safety.

As the sun goes down behind the mature pines on the crest of the hill the Pitchwood ponies are grazing as usual.

The only time the ponies do not have their heads down in the grass is when they are lying down asleep. Twiggy, Tootsie and Dresden are dozing off. Millie is flat out, sound asleep.

Ponies are much better than humans at remembering places, and their talent for finding their way home, even across strange country, is almost uncanny, and to this day largely unexplained. They may well be sensitive to the Earth's magnetic field and navigate by reference to magnetic north and south, as pigeons and some other animals do. They certainly use scents to help them and their mental maps will help them orientate themselves in relation to visible landmarks. Their talent has been little studied, but there seems no doubt that many ponies can find their way home over a long distance even through countryside they have never before seen or smelled. Whatever the explanation, many a lost rider has cause to be thankful to the pony that had no doubt about the shortest route back home. Their skill has real value to the ponies themselves, who may need to find their way back to the main herd over unfamiliar territory.

No matter how small it may be, once a new range has been explored each of the ponies starts choosing its own particular places within it for particular activities. Perhaps this is part of its mapping, rather like the way people arriving in a new neighbourhood might seek out the best or most convenient shops. There is a place for most things, and ponies, like people, soon settle to an orderly life.

A pony will find places where it prefers to feed, others where it loafs and dozes. It will have favourite spots to roll, to play, to sleep, and to dung. Even if all it has is a tiny paddock, a pony will try to find a special place for every part of its routine and once the places have been identified the pony will keep to them. If the range is large enough there will be more than one spot for most activities, to allow for moving around and for changes in the weather. One place might be very pleasant for a doze in the sun, for example, but miserable when it pours with rain.

As night fell over their new range the ponies lay down to rest in their small groups. They did not sleep through the night. From time to time they would get up, move around a little, graze, and then lie down again, and they were up and ready for a new day as the first light appeared.

Millie and Dresden look up briefly, but Porcelain goes on grazing. There is a heavy dew on the grass as the first glimmer of sunrise shows through a break in the clouds just before dawn.

Young and independent

At six months old, Dresden is no longer a baby. He is a young colt, and not part of a large herd any more. With a small group of his peers he is rapidly gaining experience of his world to equip him for adult life. New adventures await him at a time of year that would have presented a testing ordeal for a wild colt.

Summer is giving way to autumn. Leaves are beginning to fall and the grass is growing more slowly. Soon all plant growth will cease and without feeding from humans the ponies will have to survive the cold of winter with no more sustenance than they can find among the tough, poor, wilting grass and the year's growth on such evergreen trees and shrubs as they can reach. When it snows, even the grass and herbs will be hidden from them.

For Dresden, who does not go hungry, the snow will be something new that transforms the entire world. It brings new smells, new sounds, new sights, and new opportunities to play. He runs and kicks his heels in joy.

Dresden has been put all by himself in the front paddock for the day. He runs around restlessly, calling out to ponies in the other fields whom he can see, but cannot herd with. He is alone for the first time in his life, and he does not like it. He is almost too unhappy to eat.

Growing in experience

As the young ponies grew bigger, their games increasingly expressed and reinforced the social relationships among them. There was some bullying. This is common, probably more so among domesticated ponies than those that live wild, and it is very similar to bullying among children. The bully is not senior to the victim socially, is not superior, and indeed may suffer from some psychological insecurity. The bully is just a bully, and bullying foals are often the offspring of bullying mares.

Porcelain was a gentle mare, not assertive, and she tended to be a victim. This may have isolated her from groups that included her tormenters, and since Dresden always stayed close to her while he was small, it may explain why he seemed slow to make friends.

When he grew bigger he inherited his mother's temperament and became a second-generation victim. The bullying was not serious, never amounted to a full-blooded fight, but bullying seldom does. The bully needs victims, but prefers to avoid ponies, or people, who stand up and fight.

So Dresden had to endure teasing nips rather than bites. Percy, the aggressor, would approach holding his ears erect and facing forwards. He was alert but not genuinely angry, and though he turned his back defensively, Dresden simply walked

Percy taking a little nip at Dresden's hock. His upright ears show that he is only teasing. If he had really meant to bully, he would have laid his ears flat back, aggressively.

Diary · Six months

Dresden had been weaned several weeks ago. Porcelain was losing condition, so Dresden was taken away early. He had accepted separation from his mother because he had had Millie for company; she had been weaned from Mena at the same time. But then Millie had been taken away to her new home; and for three days Dresden was all by himself. The two other foals, Percy and Prince, were being weaned, but could not be put out in the paddock with him yet in case they tried to jump out. But today they have settled down enough to go out.

Prince teasing again. Dresden starts out of the way as the black foal's rump swings towards him. His tight mouth shows anxiety, but Prince's ears are only listening backwards.

away. Percy may merely have been practising his herding technique. He held his head low, quite like a herding stallion, and in a foolish position for an attack. It was dangerously close to a hind hoof that could strike him very hard, and too fast for him to avoid it.

Mares are more likely than stallions to retaliate with kicks from the hind legs. A stallion usually confronts his foes and, if necessary, rears at them. Perhaps Percy knows he is safe because if Dresden were prepared to fight back that is probably how he would do it. Dresden was not a fighter by nature, though. His response to a taunt or possible challenge was to move out of the way to avoid a confrontation.

It was a trying time for all the young ponies, because when they were six months old they were weaned. They had been grazing and browsing most of their lives, of course, but a wild pony continues to suckle until it is a year old and its mother has started feeding her next foal. It receives little milk during the later months, but everything helps and the young animal has to grow as rapidly as possible and build up bodily food reserves to see it through its first winter. Humans manage things differently for domesticated animals. A young pony will not go hungry in winter because extra food will always be available. This makes early weaning possible and at the same time allows the pregnant mare to devote all her food to feeding herself and the new foal she is carrying. This ensures the health of the mare and the new foal, but it is not popular.

Diary · Six months

While Percy and Prince grazed, Dresden visited his father's dung heap. (The colts had the paddock for the mornings, Fidelity in the afternoons.) The heap was in a muddy, much trampled corner under a big tree. Dresden spent a long time carefully smelling yesterday's dung and pawing it, then had a good roll in the mud. No doubt this made him smell big and stalliony!

Dresden rolling in a muddy corner beside his father's dung heap. On his feet again, he shakes himself like a dog far right.

The young ponies have no wish to be weaned, even though they do not really need their occasional drinks of milk. When a mare misses conceiving and there is no new foal, the old foal will happily go on suckling for a second year. The only way to wean a youngster that does not wish to be weaned is to separate it from its mother. Both mares and foals find the forced separation distressing. They can become very unhappy indeed if they have no company.

Dresden was not short of company and soon adjusted to the new situation. He was able to look after himself. The early autumn rain made mud, as an aid to grooming. After sniffing it carefully first, he rolled luxuriantly in its cool, soothing softness, easing away all the itches and insect bites from his back and dislodging the loose hair, then shook himself violently to rid his coat of the mud and the rubbish that had stuck to it. It is a highly efficient way to take a bath.

He had watched the adults roll in this way many times, and Dresden was a natural mimic. The youngsters learned by imitating others and even imitated one another.

The rain also made puddles, strange new shapes and textures on the ground that had to be examined carefully but cautiously. A pony cannot see what is directly beneath its head and the ground to each side, on which it stands, is out of focus. When he wished to look closely at something at ground level Dresden had to move to one side of it and lower his head a little.

He could smell the water and would drink readily enough from a puddle, delicately sucking the clean surface water from which soil particles had settled out, but he would not walk through the puddle if there was a way round it. Since he could not see precisely where he was treading he could never be sure that the water was not covering a hole or soft ground, where a

Diary · Six months

There had been a lot of rain during the last week, so the paddock was quite boggy in places; the underlying brick clay prevented the water draining away. Dresden was quite unconcerned about puddles now. When he had been alone in the paddock he had raced up and down the fence through the biggest puddle whenever any ponies were led past, more anxious for their company than mindful of where he was putting his feet. Today he slopped nonchalantly through the water, whereas Prince and Percy were still very wary of it.

Within the confines of his home paddock Dresden gives a passable imitation of a Carmague pony sending up the spray.

102

false step might trap or trip him. So at first he was cautious, but the ground was sodden and he soon learned he could walk through puddles safely.

Ponies can be trained to overcome their fear of walking through water, coming eventually to trust that their human companions will guide them away from danger. Unless they have been trained, however, they will not gallop confidently through shallow rivers as they do in western movies, and while they may enjoy a good gallop along a sandy beach nothing will tempt them to splash along the edge of the sea. Their fear is of the ground on which they tread rather than the water itself, and they will swim if they must.

Dresden, drinking from the rain puddle, sucks up the clean surface layer without disturbing the sedimented silt. The colts apparently ignored the windfall apples, not recognizing them as food. Older ponies know what apples are, and would have shown the foals.

Diary · Seven months

Percy did not seem happy this morning. He rolled a few times and was very restless. He followed the other two and tried to graze, but hardly ate a blade, just nosed the grass. Then he walked away to the other end of the paddock and stood by himself with his back to the sun.

As the grass became older and tougher the ponies began looking for tastier foods. Adult ponies are wary of trying anything new and it is difficult to introduce them to unfamiliar foods even if these are tasty and highly nutritious, although if they are hungry enough ponies of any age are likely to eat yew, which is very poisonous indeed. Youngsters, on the other hand, are prepared to try most things. It would have been easy to teach Dresden and his friends to eat foods that are not part of a normal pony diet. In some countries ponies learn to eat cooked meat.

Unfortunately, their sense of adventure and experiment can lead young animals to eat items that are bad for them. They will gorge on acorns, for example, and may poison themselves. Acorns are nutritious and harmless in small amounts, but in autumn when they fall to the ground in abundance and lie there just for the picking, a pony may go too far. They are rich in carbohydrates, but very bitter and astringent, and if it eats more than just a few of them the pony will suffer a badly upset stomach. The complaint soon passes, and is seldom serious, but while it lasts the victim feels very uncomfortable.

The colts engaged rowdily in mock battles. These were friendly contests, with ears erect and mouths closed, but they were also rehearsals for the fierce and terrifying battles that are occasionally fought between stallions.

Real battles are rare among wild stallions. They may erupt suddenly, with almost no warning. The combatants may then

fight until one of them is badly injured or even dead.

In a real fight their weapons would be their teeth. The youngsters played at trying to bite one another in the throat, each of them rearing partly to get out of reach and partly so he could come down heavily on the opponent and throw him to the ground where he would be helpless. They tried to nip one another at the elbow because a bite there makes a pony draw the injured leg back towards the body, throwing him off balance. They pushed and barged, and danced around one another between bouts, looking for openings.

Diary · Seven months

Percy looked like Porcelain, the evening she was in labour. His head was up, not in the relaxed dozing position, but uncomfortably high. Every now and then he tensed his head back further, as she had done, then looked round, first at one flank, then at the other. Occasionally he passed almost pure water, wetting his hind legs so they glistened. But it was better he was scouring than constipated, because Percy had made a pig of himself over fallen acorns the day before, and had eaten too many of the mildly toxic seeds. Luckily, they had not given him real colic, just some discomfort. But it was a couple of days before he had ridded his system of the toxins and was eating properly again.

Far left top, Percy standing with his head pulled back, looking most uncomfortable. He is in no mood for play, so Prince has a sparring match with Dresden, far left bottom. They prance around left, rearing up and boxing with their front feet – two little colts playing at being big stallions fighting.

105

Coping with cold

We had arranged to move Dresden from Pitchwood over to Glendale again, to the indoor riding school. We hoped to try for action shots of him against a black background, and this would have to be done indoors. We very much doubted if we would ever be able to induce a headstrong colt foal like Dresden even to walk where we wanted him, let alone display his other paces in the right place. However, we had agreed to try. So Dresden was brought over in a horsebox and turned out into the Glendale nursery paddock, which had good stallion fencing. The Glendale horses were intrigued by the newcomer and there was much sniffing of noses over the fence and excited milling around. Of course, Dresden could not be allowed to mix with strange horses and ponies without proper introductions over the fence first. It was hoped that he would eventually pal up with a Welsh gelding, Sundance Apollo (Titch), a really steady character, mature and kind, who would not only be his friend at Glendale, but act as the carrot to make Dresden go where we wanted him for the action shots indoors. The two ponies were interested in each other straightaway. They ran along the fence together, sniffed noses through it, and pretended to graze with heads close. Then Titch would saunter away as if totally disinterested, graze a bit, but suddenly rush back at Dresden with his ears back. Both would swing round rump to rump, so there might have been a few kicks exchanged had the fence not been between them.

Below *Getting to know one another through the fence – Dresden mouthing as Titch smells his muzzle.*

Far right *Dresden with snow blanket on his back and crystals on his whiskers.*

In January, rapidly and without warning, a tongue of Asian air extended itself westward across Europe and overnight the cool, damp, British winter gave way to weather that was almost arctic. Ponds and rivers froze, blizzards raged, and still the temperatures fell.

Dresden saw snow for the first time. Like children, ponies often greet the first snow of winter with enthusiasm. They run and frolic and roll in it. At first Dresden seemed rather indifferent, however, perhaps because the ground beneath the snow was uninviting. Much trampling had made it uneven and then it had frozen hard.

The cold did not trouble him, provided it was not too windy and he could keep dry. Wild ponies live and thrive on the steppes of central Asia, the source of the cold British weather; and in North America, where the descendants of ponies introduced by humans live wild, winters are no less severe. With a large, bulky body to generate heat, and a relatively small surface area through which to lose it, a pony has little difficulty in keeping warm. In winter it grows a thick coat, shedding the surplus in summer. Blood vessels just below the skin contract in cold weather. This restricts the flow of blood from deep inside the body to the surface. It allows the skin to cool while keeping the vital internal organs warm.

With his feet covered by snow, and ice on his whiskers, Dresden would have felt very cold to touch, but he was not in the least uncomfortable.

Diary · Nine months

It had snowed quite a lot overnight. I had expected Dresden to be all excited about it when he was put out in the morning. But he didn't even roll in it! The ground beneath the snow had been cut up by the horses' hoofs and was now frozen, so was uncomfortable to run or roll on. The only thing any of the horses wanted to do was to get at the grass underneath the snow.

The older animals paw the snow to get at the grass, but Dresden pushes it away with his muzzle as he grazes. Then he rubs the frozen snow from his face against his foreleg.

A light breeze might have encouraged him to play, but had he been wet, or had there been a strong wind, he would have sought shelter, at the very least standing with his back to the wind. Wind and water conduct heat away from the body and its resistance to cold is overcome. Chilled, he would soon have begun to shiver.

Despite their ability to withstand low temperatures, winter remains a testing time for ponies living in the wild and many die. Plant growth ceases. Most herbs disappear, deciduous trees and bushes lose their leaves, and grasses lie dormant, their nutritive value at its lowest. Food is scarce, just when extra is needed to combat the cold, and water is frozen. It is a time of hunger and thirst.

The predators, too, are hungrier, for many prey animals have disappeared for the winter into burrows, some to hibernate, others to spend most of their time sleeping. Wolves that hunt singly in summer and live well on abundant supplies of small animals, in winter hunt larger game and work in packs. A herd of ponies, some enfeebled by privation, moving slowly and

conspicuously across a white landscape, is an obvious target. Just when they are at a low ebb, their vigilance must increase.

Snow hides food, but a pony can paw it away with a hoof. Dresden preferred a different technique. He pushed the snow away with his muzzle as he grazed, then wiped the snow off his face against his foreleg. At least one pony has been seen to use a stick to rake away snow. It is one of the few examples of a pony using a tool.

Survival in winter depends mainly on eating well while food is plentiful. A foal born in spring has eight to ten months in which to grow large enough to withstand intense cold, to lay down reserves of fat on which its body can draw in emergencies, and to develop the strength and stamina to remain active and vigilant through the hard times.

Dresden was still a foal, weaned from his mother, contentedly spending all of his time with his friends. His physical development was not yet complete, and his training had hardly begun, but he was persuaded to canter by himself under controlled conditions in an indoor riding school.

Diary · Nine months

Titch was turned out into the nursery paddock with Dresden today. There was a little skirmishing and threatening with ears back, but Titch was unshod and anyway such a gentleman that no blows were struck. Another pony, the dapple-grey mare Nanturrian Pride and Joy, was also keen to be friends with Dresden.

In spite of the winter weather Joy has come in season and is flirting with Dresden. He flehms after smelling her urine. Perhaps it is as well the nursery paddock has stallion fencing!

The ponies in action

A pony can progress at a walk, trot, canter or gallop. The first three of these gaits are quite distinct and there is a clear change in the pony's action as it switches from one to another. The transition from canter to gallop is, by contrast, a smooth progression. A pony also has a marked ability to jump, not only on its own, but carrying a rider as well. To show how some of these actions are accomplished, multiple-image photography has been used. The equipment was set up in the riding school and the ponies slowly introduced to a situation that involved a noisily clicking camera accompanied by brilliantly flashing lights. Dresden had experienced photo flash since birth and was completely immune to it. Titch and Joy, on the other hand, were somewhat nervous and had to be very gently acclimatized. Joy eventually became the star, showing her paces and jumping unfalteringly in front of the camera.

It was photography at the end of the last century which showed conclusively how a horse moves its feet in each of the four gaits. Until then it was the fashion for artists to paint galloping horses with legs outstretched as if they were bounding through the air, but while a horse is in suspension its legs are tucked beneath it, not outstretched. At full speed, a horse can be in suspension for up to one-third of the time. As it comes down, the horse lands on its hind feet, then rocks on to its forefeet before taking off again. This action contrasts with that of other animals such as antelopes, cheetahs and dogs, which bound from the hind feet and land forefeet first. The walk is another gait that has variations. Most animals, including horses, move diagonally opposite feet at the same time when walking. But some like elephants and giraffes, move fore and hind feet on the same side in unison. This is called ambling. Some dogs do it naturally, and horses can be taught to do it.

Dresden shows his paces

Training a pony off the rein requires skill and time; it also requires a pony that is ready to be trained. Although Dresden is used to a head collar and can be led without too many problems he is really too young for serious training. He is a headstrong young colt, and to persuade him to show his paces in front of the camera required careful management. Dresden resolutely ignored any carrots waved in his direction during his first experience in the riding school and seemed much more interested in investigating his surroundings. He was also unsettled because he was separated from his great friend Titch, and whinnied anxiously. On subsequent occasions, Titch was brought into the school with Dresden and the two were led around together. Then, while Dresden's attention was diverted, Titch was led off at a smart pace past the camera. The sound of his hoofs seemed to act as a catalyst and Dresden unfailingly sprang into action to follow. If Titch was led away slowly, however, Dresden just watched him go. It seemed as if the herd instinct was aroused in Dresden more by the sound of hoofs than by the sight of his friend moving away. For the purpose of photography it was Titch's job to act as a carrot. Dresden is seen (left) chasing after Titch during a training session to get them both used to the situation in the riding school. He canters after Titch (below) whose disappearing tail is just visible.

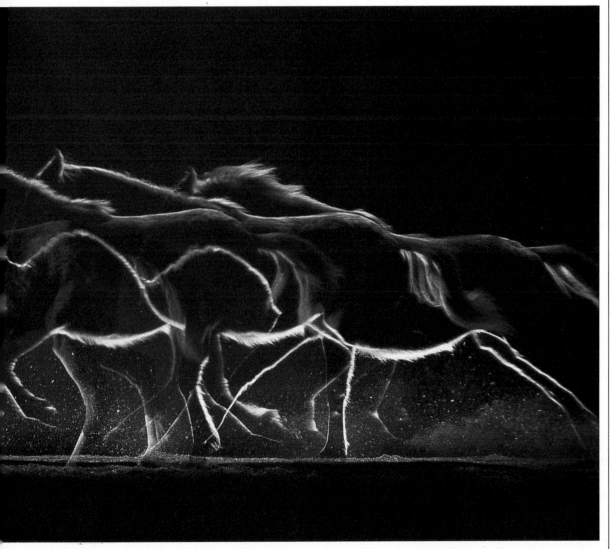

Walking

When a horse walks, the sound of its footfall forms a regular beat in 4-time. There are four steps to a stride, with each leg being moved independently in regular sequence and never more than two hoofs off the ground at a time. As the right forefoot is brought forward, the left hind foot is lifted off the ground and as this is brought forward, the right forefoot is placed on the ground. The latter stage can be seen most clearly in the first (right hand) image of this sequence of Joy walking. By chance the four images are spaced at exactly half stride intervals so that the first and third are identical, and so are the second and fourth. In fact all four images represent the stage in the stride when both forefeet are more or less on the ground while one hind foot is being brought past the other. The placing of the hind feet in relation to the prints left by the forefeet depends on the length of the stride. In an 'extended walk' the hind feet fall in front of the prints left by the forefeet, whereas in a 'collected walk' the hind feet fall behind the fore footprints. When the prints coincide, it is known as 'tracking up'. Here Joy is walking sedately, with the neck arched and head held almost vertically. She is exhibiting a 'collected walk' and it can be seen that her hind feet are falling just short of the positions vacated by her forefeet.

Young and independent

Trotting

The footfall of a trotting horse forms a regular beat in 2-time. Diagonally opposite feet are moved in unison, with moments of suspension when all four feet are off the ground. The second (from the right) of the four images shown here of Joy trotting comes nearest to capturing the moment of suspension. Right fore and left hind foot are just about to strike the ground while their opposite numbers are just being picked up. Without a moment of suspension it would be impossible for a trotting horse to place its hind feet in the prints of its forefeet; it would kick its own feet. But, as all four feet leave the ground together the horse is travelling forward so that 'tracking up' is possible in trotting as well as in walking.

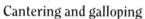

Cantering and galloping

The sound of a cantering horse forms a beat in 3-time. The order in which the feet are moved is the same as that in the walk, but there is a period of suspension during each stride. The horse takes off from a forefoot and lands first on a diagonally opposite hind foot. The other two feet strike the ground in quick succession, forming the middle beat.

Galloping is a much more energetic action. The period of suspension is longer and there are never more than two feet on the ground at a time. Here, Joy's rider is urging her forward as quickly as possible in the limited space available within the riding school. The fourth image of the sequence illustrates the period of suspension. Joy has just taken off from her left forefoot which can be seen firmly on the ground in the preceding image. Her right hind foot is poised to strike the ground at the start of another stride.

114

Young and independent

Jumping

The sequence (right) shows Joy clearing a low fence. She has not quite got the measure of it and falters momentarily before taking off, leading with her left forefoot which is not her favourite. As she clears the fence, both forefeet come together and by the time she lands, she is leading with her right. But even before her hind feet touch the ground, the right forefoot is leading off for another stride. She has jumped higher and further than necessary to clear the fence. Experienced show-jumping ponies have a remarkable ability to judge visually the height and width of a jump so that minimum effort is expended in clearing each obstacle. But Joy can be excused any errors; the unusual circumstances of flashing lights and clicking camera are enough to put off most horses altogether.

After clearing the fence several times, Joy is presented with a bar on the ground in front of the fence. She is taken by surprise and refuses, throwing her rider forward.

Young and independent

Jumping for joy

Ponies can be trained to alter their paces on verbal command. This can be done with a riderless pony on a long rein known as a lunge line. Jumping on command is a step forward from this. Joy is used to a rider but surprised everyone by showing her willingness to jump riderless. Without previous training she was just pointed in the right direction and happily cleared the fence many times on her own. It seemed as if she wanted to show off but it is possible that she enjoyed the freedom of jumping without the additional weight of a rider. Ponies can carry, and jump with, a rider who adds as much as ten per cent to their weight. This is equivalent to an athlete weighing 140lb (60k) competing with a 14lb (6k) weight strapped to his or her back. Here Joy is totally unfettered and clears the fence with ease and grace.

A new generation

Diary · One year

Much had happened at Pitchwood Stud since Dresden's return from Glendale two months ago. Before the first foals had begun to arrive, the show season had already got underway. The Pitchwood ponies did extremely well at their first shows. Fidelity continued to make Champion Stallion and Supreme Champion. Barbie, Tootsie and young Whisky (back for showing and looking gorgeous) had been first in their classes at several shows.

Dresden and his two childhood companions, Percy and Prince, no longer played together in the front paddock, but had to be turned out separately for their daily run around and roll in the mud. Their boxing matches had become so rough they had started cutting up each other's faces and shoulders with their hoofs. Colts can really injure one another, to the extent of breaking bones, so these violent play bouts had to cease.

Now the new batch of Pitchwood foals were a week or so old. Brandy, mother of Whisky, was again the first to foal-down this year, with a pretty little bay filly. Filumena, back at Pitchwood for the summer, had another filly foal like last year's Millie. Porcelain had not given birth yet, like last year, she would be very late to foal. Her old enemy Peepshine gave birth to a strapping chestnut colt. Soubrette, Prince's mother, was resting this year. So there were three foals already scampering in the nursery paddock. This spring had been unusually warm and sunny, in contrast to the dreary late spring when Dresden had been born.

Just like last year Porcelain is playing the waiting game, keeping us in suspense. Her foal is two weeks overdue already. Her foal will probably be another colt; filly foals often arrive early while colt foals arrive late.

Dresden's new half-brother is so huge, with legs already almost as long as his mother, Peepshine. He has been nick-named Thomas the Tank. Only days old, he is already exploring and charging around the paddock.

The yearling

I hardly recognised Dresden 'the show pony' as the same animal I had last seen. He was then all whiskery and covered in mud, slopping through the rain and puddles in the front paddock on his first birthday. He had matured late, like all Fidelity's foals, so had not been ready for showing at the beginning of the season. But when I photographed him yesterday he had finished moulting, had put on extra weight, and he was being prepared for his first show. He is a potential champion, like both his parents. His coat will probably darken to liver chestnut, like Fidelity's, by the time he is a three-year-old.

Today I heard that Dresden had won a red rosette! At a county show he was placed first in a class of colt, filly, and gelding yearlings that will not exceed 13.2hh at maturity. Time will tell whether he will ever wear the Supreme Champion's sash like his father.

Right *A high-spirited colt will stand for only so much of this tedious posing. There are mares in the fields, spring greenery all around, and many exciting sights and smells to make him restless.*

Below *With his plaited mane and show bridle as polished as his chestnut summer coat, Dresden looks a little winner. After weeks of training he stands still with untypical patience for his official portrait.*

Dresden's progress - an extended summary

We have followed Dresden through the first year of his life, and end the book by summarizing that year. The summary relates Dresden's development to that of a wild colt at the same age, living in a herd.

Then we move forward in the same way, to predict Dresden's future and that of a wild pony, in the years to come.

The first year

The beginning
Dresden was born in the small hours of an April morning. A wild mare would find somewhere solitary to give birth, often near water. The birth itself was very quick. Dresden was born with his eyes and ears open and functioning. By the time he was two hours old he could stand, walk a short distance, and was feeding.

1 week to 1 month
Porcelain kept her foal beside her, and he followed wherever she went, safe within her personal space. Dresden continued exploring his surroundings, mainly with his nose and mouth, but he did a lot of looking too. He perfected the technique for lying down and standing up, and also for trotting, cantering and galloping.

1 month to 3 months
Dresden and his mother communicated using basic greetings, facial expressions, and body postures all ponies use with one another. As he grew larger and more self-confident he began to wander further from her, though never out of her sight, and to meet other ponies. He began to make friends among the foals.

3 months to 6 months
As summer advanced, Dresden grew even more playful; a member of a group of foals. In the wild, colts would have begun to play together in groups while the fillies tended to stay close to their mothers. But even the colts never wandered far from the protection of the herd. Close friendships are often formed at this age.

6 months to 9 months
By this time most domesticated foals are weaned. It can be a distressing time because mothers and foals are separated unwillingly. Wild foals do not need the milk, but continue to suckle until a new foal is born. Dresden had friends to keep him company after weaning, and soon adjusted to the new situation.

9 months to 1 year
As winter approaches, with cooler weather and a dwindling food supply, wild ponies begin to move, searching for better grazing. Dresden was safe and well fed, and increasingly interested in exploring, but also large enough and strong enough to have kept up with the adults, even if they had had to flee from danger.

The years to come

Year 2	As a yearling, during the summer Dresden will be shown in yearling classes, where he will be judged for general appearance and movement and suitability as a pony for a child. Later in the year a decision will be	made either to geld him or keep him to become a stallion, for breeding. When the show season ends he will continue to live outdoors, coming inside only at night when the weather is bad.
Year 3	In the wild, a two-year old will remain with the herd, although he and his friends play less and are moving further away in their explorations. Dresden will begin training, with short lunging sessions, and	will be shown during the summer. At the end of the show season he will be turned out for a complete rest for a few weeks until preparations begin for the next show season.
Year 4	Three-year old colts in the wild explore away from their own herd. In the course of their travels they may meet another herd, and join it. For Dresden, lunging will continue, but now it will be in	preparation for breaking him. He will be backed, and then ridden. In summer he may be shown in novice classes; a pony suitable for riding by someone under 14 years of age.
Year 5	At four, a colt is settling down. He spends most of his time with the herd, ready for the day when he has mares of his own. He will be fully adult by the time he is five. Dresden will continue to be shown in	novice classes for another year but then, if he attains a really high standard in a year or two, he might qualify to be entered in the Pony of the Year class at the Horse of the Year Show.

Pony Club Headquarters

GREAT BRITAIN (366 branches)
Pony Club and British Horse Society
British Equestrian Centre
Stoneleigh
Kenilworth
Warwickshire CV8 2LR

British Show Pony Society
C/o Mrs J. Toynton
124 Green End Road
Sawtry
Huntingdon
Cambridgeshire

UNITED STATES
U.S Pony Clubs Inc
C/o Miss S. Giddings
893 Matlack Street
Suite 110
West Chester
Pennsylvania 19382

CANADA
Canadian Pony Clubs Inc
C/o Mrs M. MacDonald
Box 7
Site 17
Rural Route 5
Calgary
Alberta T2P 2G6

AUSTRALIA
Pony Club Council
C/o Mrs Brideoake
Box 46
Lockheart 2656
New South Wales

NEW ZEALAND
Pony Club Association Inc
C/o Mrs Wakeling
Kaitieke
RD2 Owhango
King Country

Index

Page numbers in italic refer to photographs

AUTHORS' NOTE

Jane Burton and Kim Taylor would like to acknowledge their thanks to:

Dee Bennet for her interest and willing cooperation in the whole project throughout the year; Peggy and Bill Lucas for allowing us to come and go at Pitchwood Stud, Ewhurst, Surrey, and especially Peggy for sharing the night watches and alerting us to the imminent arrival of the foal; Pat Bennett, the owner of Porcelain and Dresden; and Tracy Wilson, the Pitchwood Stud groom, for cheerfully washing mud off ponies!

We would also like to thank: Carolyn Woods for her enthusiasm and generosity in allowing us to use the special facilities at 'Glendale', Farley Green, Surrey; Jenny Woods and her pony, Joy, for accomplishing the impossible; and Lynsey Ness for her special care of Dresden at 'Glendale'.

In addition we thank: Norman Thomas for allowing us to put ponies in his field; Francis Burton for reading the text and for his helpful suggestions in interpreting pony behaviour; Susan Chitty for neatly typing our almost unreadable scrawl; and Nick Eddison for bullying us into attempting the impossible!

ACKNOWLEDGEMENTS

Editorial Director	Ian Jackson
Creative Director	Nick Eddison
Designer	Amanda Barlow
Editor	Christine Moffat
Copy Editor and Proofreader	Geraldine Christy
Indexer	Michael Allaby
Production	Bob Towell